1991

Involving Adults in the Educational Process

Sandra H. Rosenblum, *Editor*   W9-DGV-633

NEW DIRECTIONS FOR CONTINUING EDUCATION

GORDON G. DARKENWALD, *Editor-in-Chief*
ALAN B. KNOX, *Consulting Editor*

Number 26, June 1985

Paperback sourcebooks in
The Jossey-Bass Higher Education Series

Jossey-Bass Inc., Publishers
San Francisco • London

Sandra H. Rosenblum (Ed.).
Involving Adults in the Educational Process.
New Directions for Continuing Education, no. 26.
San Francisco: Jossey-Bass, 1985.

New Directions for Continuing Education Series
Gordon G. Darkenwald, *Editor-in-Chief*
Alan B. Knox, *Consulting Editor*

New Directions for Continuing Education (publication number
USPS 493-930) quarterly by Jossey-Bass Inc., Publishers.
Second-class postage rates paid at San Francisco, California,
and at additional mailing offices.

Correspondence:
Subscriptions, single-issue orders, change of address notices, undelivered
copies, and other correspondence should be sent to Subscriptions,
Jossey-Bass Inc., Publishers, 433 California Street, San Francisco,
California 94104.

Editorial correspondence should be sent to the managing
Editor-in-Chief, Gordon G. Darkenwald, Graduate School
of Education, Rutgers University, 10 Seminary Place,
New Brunswick, New Jersey 08903.

Library of Congress Catalogue Card Number LC 84-82369
International Standard Serial Number ISSN 0195-2242
International Standard Book Number ISBN 87589-744-4

Cover art by Willi Baum
Manufactured in the United States of America

Ordering Information

The paperback sourcebooks listed below are published quarterly and can be ordered either by subscription or single-copy.

Subscriptions cost $35.00 per year for institutions, agencies, and libraries. Individuals can subscribe at the special rate of $25.00 per year *if payment is by personal check.* (Note that the full rate of $35.00 applies if payment is by institutional check, even if the subscription is designated for an individual.) Standing orders are accepted. Subscriptions normally begin with the first of the four sourcebooks in the current publication year of the series. When ordering, please indicate if you prefer your subscription to begin with the first issue of the *coming* year.

Single copies are available at $8.95 when payment accompanies order, and *all single-copy orders under $25.00 must include payment.* (California, New Jersey, New York, and Washington, D.C., residents please include appropriate sales tax.) For billed orders, cost per copy is $8.95 plus postage and handling. (Prices subject to change without notice.)

Bulk orders (ten or more copies) of any individual sourcebook are available at the following discounted prices: 10–49 copies, $8.05 each; 50–100 copies, $7.15 each; over 100 copies, *inquire.* Sales tax and postage and handling charges apply as for single copy orders.

To ensure correct and prompt delivery, all orders must give either the *name of an individual* or an *official purchase order number.* Please submit your order as follows:

Subscriptions: specify series and year subscription is to begin.
Single Copies: specify sourcebook code (such as, CE8) and first two words of title.

Mail orders for United States and Possessions, Latin America, Canada, Japan, Australia, and New Zealand to:
    Jossey-Bass Inc., Publishers
    433 California Street
    San Francisco, California 94104

Mail orders for all other parts of the world to:
    Jossey-Bass Limited
    28 Banner Street
    London EC1Y 8QE

New Directions for Continuing Education Series
Gordon G. Darkenwald, *Editor-in-Chief*
Alan B. Knox, Consulting Editor

CE1 *Enhancing Proficiencies of Continuing Educators,* Alan B. Knox
CE2 *Programming for Adults Facing Mid-Life Change,* Alan B. Knox
CE3 *Assessing the Impact of Continuing Education,* Alan B. Knox
CE4 *Attracting Able Instructors of Adults,* M. Alan Brown, Harlan G. Copeland

Contents

Editor's Notes

It is a serious error for continuing educators to ignore the enormously rich resources that adults bring to a learning situation. Adult learners can be treated as passive agents who simply soak up information directed at them, or they can be called upon to share their thinking, knowledge, and experience with the instructor and with one another. Creating an environment where only one in a group of adults, the instructor, assumes sole control over the learning process diminishes the learning situation for everyone involved, learners and instructor alike.

The contributors to this sourcebook believe that the most significant learning occurs when adult students and their instructors together plan the learning process and together participate in carrying it out. Consequently, in a variety of ways, this volume of *New Directions for Continuing Education* explores the topic of how continuing educators can successfully involve their adult students in the educational process.

In Chapter One, John Niemi discusses the fostering of student participation in learning, where interaction occurs between learner and teacher, between learner and peers, and between learner and nonhuman resources.

Chapter Two reviews the literature on the adult's role in educational planning and discusses the effect of such involvement on educational outcomes.

In Chapter Three, Kathy Vedros introduces us to a technique for enhancing student involvement in planning. She describes the nominal group technique, a structured process that enables adults to participate actively in planning their learning activities.

Paul Ilsley examines the constraints on student involvement in literacy programs in Chapter Four. The constraints are caused by the tensions between the "culture of professionalism" and the "culture of illiteracy." He recommends some ways of increasing student participation.

Unique challenges and problems exist in a learning situation where student and instructor are separated by many miles. In Chapter Five, Michael Law and Linda Sissons suggest that technologies can be developed to maximize dialogue and learner autonomy in distance education.

In Chapter Six, Stephen Brookfield critically evaluates discussion as a participative method in continuing education and presents recommendations to ensure its most successful use.

Michael Law and Linda Sissons explore adult education as a vehicle for social change in Chapter Seven. The authors contend that the key question for continuing educators is not only how we can involve others in social change education but how we as educators can usefully involve ourselves in social change.

Chapter Eight takes us into the world of cultural institutions, where David Carr stresses the importance to meaningful learning of the relationship between the "guide" and the adult learner in such settings as museums and libraries.

In Chapter Nine, Jonathan Freedman, in a personal vein, shares strategies and techniques to encourage learner participation that have worked for him during many years of teaching adults.

Chapter Ten focuses on the alteration that must occur in educator-student roles in order for the adult learner to become central to the planning-learning process.

Sandra H. Rosenblum
Editor

Sandra H. Rosenblum is director of education and training at the New York State Psychiatric Institute and instructor of clinical psychiatry at Columbia University. She also teaches in the graduate program in adult and continuing education at Rutgers University, and she is a consulting editor of Adult Education Quarterly.

Participation by adults in their own learning can be fostered whether that learning occurs in the institutional mode, the shared membership mode, or the individual mode.

Fostering Participation in Learning

John A. Niemi

Much research has been done on participation in continuing education programs, in the sense of who participates and of what motivates people to do so. This chapter focuses on participation in the learning process. Although the act of learning is an internal phenomenon, it comes about through interaction between the learner and other human beings or nonhuman entities or forces. This observable involvement of the learner in his or her own learning is what is meant by participation. Little (1979) pointed out that learning can take place in a societal setting (learning by chance) or in a continuing education setting (learning by design). This chapter discusses the fostering of participation in the continuing education setting, where there is interaction between learner and teacher, between learner and peers, or between learner and nonhuman resources, such as books, computers, radio, or television (sometimes in combination with a human resource).

Blaney's model (1974) of curriculum formation offers a useful framework for examining participation as it relates to the role of the teacher, the role of the learner, and the transactions that take place between them in the learning process. However, before we proceed, we need to review the unique characteristics of adult learners, because they have a significant bearing on the learning process.

S. H. Rosenblum (Ed.). *Involving Adults in the Educational Process.* New Directions for Continuing Education, no. 26. San Francisco: Jossey-Bass, June 1985.

The Uniqueness of Adult Learners

In any discussion of the characteristics of adult learners, the first point that needs to be emphasized is that there is no such thing as a typical adult learner. To this blunt statement, however, can be added the qualification that certain characteristics set adult learners apart from younger learners who have pursued their formal schooling in elementary, secondary, and postsecondary institutions without interruption. As Zahn (1967, p. 67) points out, "Adults are not merely tall children. They differ from the young in many ways that influence their learning. They have different body characteristics, different learning histories, different reaction speed, different attitudes, values, interests, motivation, and personality. Therefore, those who are trying to help adults learn must be aware of these differences and adjust the teaching and learning environment accordingly."

Almost by definition, the adult learner is one who returns to study, on a full-time or part-time basis, after a period of time spent in other pursuits. As a result, he or she brings to new learning a rich background of life and work experience. This background includes the wide range of roles that adults fill: employee, spouse, parent, citizen, community or church worker. In general, then, and in contrast with younger learners, adults possess sophisticated insights springing from their knowledge of the world of work, from the skills they have acquired there, and from the relationships they have developed with other people at work and in their personal lives. These insights make it easier for them as learners to recognize how ideas can be transformed into action and how theory can be transformed into practice outside the classroom.

Another way in which adult learners differ from younger learners is that their goals are often more clear-cut. That is, adult learners are likely to identify the things that are important in their lives with some certainty—the careers to which they want to devote their energies, the skills they wish to acquire, the persons they aspire to become, or the kinds of relationships they hope to build with others. Also, adult learners are more likely to prioritize the forces competing for their attention. Of course, there are some adult learners whose goals and priorities are poorly defined.

A third way in which adult learners are likely to differ from younger ones relates to motivation, which is closely linked to goals. That is, adult learners often feel impelled to take an active part in their own learning, and they are more willing than younger learners to make sacrifices in setting goals for themselves and in striving to reach them. There are many reasons for this superior motivation. Often, adult learners are able to devote only part of their time to study because of the demands of full-time or part-time jobs and the obligations of spouse or parent. Time is very precious to them, and when they decide to devote some of it to further study they take that study seriously. Moreover, adult learners are often motivated by a desire to advance in a job or to make a career shift. Younger learners tend to take their studies less seriously.

Adult learners, then, have certain advantages, but there are problems, too. Often, they fear change and the demands placed on them by teachers who do not always comprehend the anxieties that they feel in the new situation. These anxieties are compounded in adults who have experienced failure in school and who associate learning with unpleasant memories of unsympathetic teachers, tests, low grades, and punishments. Often, they have a low self-concept, which causes them to shrink from exposing their ignorance to others and to dread further failure.

The physiological changes wrought by the aging process may also create difficulties for the pursuit of learning. These changes include deterioration of sight and hearing, loss of energy and strength, decline of memory, and a lengthening of reaction time. Clearly, not all adults age at the same rate or display the same characteristics as they age. Nevertheless, the changes (or the fear of changes) sometimes create anxieties that interfere with learning. However, there is a counterpoint to this rather dismal picture. It is the enormous adaptability of human beings who face new challenges. In the case of adult learners, their high motivation often causes them to forget their handicaps when they get caught up in the excitement of learning.

As mentioned previously, Blaney's (1974) model of curriculum formation, which is displayed in Figure 1, will be used in this chapter as a framework for its discussion of the fostering of participation as it relates to the role of the teacher, the role of the adult learner, and the transactions that take place between them in the learning process. Blaney's model presents three modes—institutional, shared membership, and individual. Each is organized according to eight program variables: authority, objectives, methods and techniques, role of the professional teacher, role of the learner, evaluation, technology, and conditions of learning.

Fostering Participation According to the Institutional Mode

Basically, the institutional mode represents content-centered adult education, wherein the most important element is the subject matter to be covered. Because the teacher's role is one of dispensing information, the authority, objectives, methods and techniques, and evaluation are all vested in the teacher. Thus, he or she assumes the

Figure 1. Modes of Curriculum Formulation and Their Relevance to Adult Education

Program Variables	Institutional Mode	Shared Membership Mode	Individual Mode
Authority	Largely external to learners; assumed and exercised by the institutions	Granted to and exercised cooperatively by learners and teacher(s)	Granted to and exercised by the individual
Objectives	Explicated prior to the instructional situation; provide the basis for planning and evaluation May be revised by teacher Consonant with controlling agency aims	May never be explicit; often evolved during learning situation and have to be inferred from group activities When explicit, more often refer to desired process than outcomes	May never be explicit but usually can be inferred from individual activity May take the form of a problem or project
Methods and Techniques	Science-based and variable; chosen in terms of assumed or demonstrated effectiveness in achieving objectives	Group-centered and process-oriented Variable and not overtly systematic	Individual-centered Variable and not overtly systematic
Role of Professional Teacher	Instructional planner and/or manager; diagnostician, motivator, and evaluator Specialists may assume some instructional tasks	As jointly determined by group members; generally as a resource person/facilitator-member	Learner assumes most teacher tasks, though may consult specialists as required Professional useful as model, supporter, and consultant
Role of Learner	Dependent role regarding objectives and evaluation To achieve prescribed objectives	Interdependent As a member who helps select ends, means, and evaluation procedures To maintain integrity of group	Independent Assumes all ends-and-means decisions Responsible for own learning
Evaluation	Generally criterion-referenced To assess effectiveness of instruction and importance of goals To improve program To diagnose learning difficulties	To determine progress toward group goals and how well group functions Generally semiformal, though often wholly subjective	Self-referenced To assess results of persistence Generally informal, often wholly subjective May be synonymous with solution of a personal problem or task
Technology	Use of "hard" and "soft" instructional technology in planning and actual instruction	Mainly application of group process theory; as determined by group	May be selected or constructed by individual for own needs
Conditions for Learning	Clear objectives and student knowledge of these; relevant practice; feedback; motivation; effective organization of learning opportunities	Positive and accepting group "climate" Full membership of learners Access to resources	Freedom to explore and take risks Access to resources, consultants, and human models

Source: Blaney, 1974, pp. 20–21.

multiple role of planner, manager, diagnostician, motivator, and eval-
uator, and the learner takes a dependent role. This highly structured
approach is appropriate in any setting where the learner must master
certain basic knowledge or skills in order to apply what has been learned
or to comprehend advanced knowledge and skills. To cite an example
from a high school equivalency class, the teacher must explain, with
illustrations, how to draw inferences from dialogue in a literary work
before the learner can engage independently in such activity. Here, it is
worth noting that Conti (1983) found that GED students learned more
in a teacher-centered environment.

Although the learner's role is dependent, it is not necessarily
passive. The institutional mode provides some opportunities for learner
participation, depending on the teacher's personal philosophy. In
stressing the importance of personal philosophy, Apps (1973) listed four
components: beliefs about the adult learner, beliefs about the purposes
of adult education, beliefs about content or subject matter, and beliefs
about the teaching-learning process. The teacher who appreciates the
unique characteristics of adult learners — their rich life experience and
the nature of their motivation and goals — may seek ways of relating
them to new learning.

The four components of a teacher's philosophy can be influenced
by learning theories that place a heavy emphasis on content. An example is behaviorism, which has been seen as an important learning theory
for training. According to Dubin and Okun (1973, p. 4), most of the
implications of Skinner's model of behaviorism deal "with the necessary
arrangement of stimuli and responses for modifying behavior." Learner
participation is limited, consisting only of responses (made at the learner's own rate) to stimuli. These responses receive immediate feedback,
which acts to reinforce the responses.

A well-known adult educator, McClusky (1973), reviewed the
standard stimulus-response formula and criticized it for its neglect of
the learner, whom he saw as the intervening variable. Concerning the
learner's participation, he wrote (p. 144) that "the raw physical proper-
ties of the stimuli are not sufficient to account for individual differences
in response." In order to delve more deeply into the teaching-learning
process under the institutional mode, we will examine learner participation as it relates to objectives, methods and techniques, and evaluation.

In the institutional mode (content-centered continuing education), the teacher formulates the objectives of instruction. Hence, if
learners do not achieve those objectives, the teacher's shortcomings,
not the learner's, are to blame (Popham, 1965). Some learners welcome

the existence of clear-cut objectives because they indicate the specific content of the course and the knowledge, skills, or attitudes that learners are expected to obtain.

Smith (1982) pointed out that formalized instruction may be important to learners for externally imposed discipline, for in-depth exploration of content, or for earning a credential. The preference of adult learners for formal approaches to learning has also been reported by Cross (1981), who cites an Educational Testing Service survey of 1972. According to that survey, 28 percent of would-be learners preferred lectures or classes, and 35 percent of enrolled learners preferred them.

In regard to methods and techniques, the institutional mode theoretically limits learner participation to listening and note taking. However, a teacher could enhance participation by asking questions and by using such techniques as group discussion to enlarge on certain concepts or principles or to discuss applications of knowledge or skills covered in the lecture.

Under the institutional mode, evaluation is based on clear-cut, criterion-referenced objectives. The objectives are used to assess the effectiveness of instruction. In essence, then, as Popham (1965) stated, objectives and evaluation are identical. Although the entire process is teacher controlled and there is no direct participation by learners, in some institutions learners participate indirectly by submitting evaluations of instruction.

Fostering Participation According to the Shared Membership Mode

The shared membership mode is either learner centered (if the focus is on clearly defined learner needs) or problem centered (if the focus is on some external need). This group-centered mode assumes collaboration and consensus between teacher and learners as they cooperatively define objectives, select methods and techniques, and conduct evaluation. Here, the teacher's role is one of resource person, coinquirer, and facilitator (Knowles, 1980). The role of facilitator was succinctly described by Lindeman ([1926] 1961, p. 119) as one whose "function is not to profess but to evoke—to draw out, not pour in." Horton's concept (Adams, 1975) of the facilitator's role was that it encourages mutual communication, raises and sharpens questions, and trusts people to find answers.

In contrast to the clear-cut instructional objectives of the institutional mode, the objectives of the shared membership mode are not always explicit, and they are frequently in flux, especially when the shared membership mode is learner centered. Knowles (1980) alluded to this quality of flux when he stressed the importance of having learners construct goals that have personal meaning for them — goals that may be terminal for some and avenues to further personal development for others. When the shared membership mode is problem centered, objectives tend to be explicit. The reason, as stated by Kidd (1973), is that the process of problem solving itself involves explicit steps: awareness that there is a problem, preparations for finding a solution, attempts to produce it, and evaluation of its adequacy.

With respect to methods and techniques in group-centered continuing education, the creation of a climate favorable to learning is of crucial importance in fostering participation. According to Knowles (1980, p. 47), this psychological climate "should be one which causes adults to feel accepted, respected, and supported; in which there exists a spirit of mutuality between teachers and students as joint inquirers; in which there is a freedom of expression without fear of punishment or ridicule." To Rogers (1969), this community of learners is one in which the teacher interacts with learners with empathy and genuine concern for individual differences.

Another important means by which learners' participation can be enhanced is incorporation of their rich background of life experience, goals, and motivation into the methods and techniques used. As Knowles (1980) asserted, learners are themselves important resources for learning. Through this means, the learning process assumes relevance for learners.

Evaluation under the shared membership mode differs sharply from evaluation under the institutional mode. Under the latter, evaluation is based on clear-cut objectives that the teacher constructs and controls. Under the shared membership mode, the purpose of evaluation is to determine how well the group has functioned and how far it has progressed toward fulfilling its objectives while meeting individual needs. However, in practice, as Smith (1982, p. 115) pointed out, learners "may take a less rigorous approach, perhaps relying on participant reaction and observation. . . . Looking for unintended outcomes can also be useful."

Fostering Participation According to the Individual Mode

The individual mode, in contrast to both the institutional mode and the shared membership modes, is entirely learner centered. The learner assumes virtually complete responsibility for the planning process. Tough (1971) coined the term *learning project* as a deliberate effort to learn through a series of related episodes. As Tough (1978) later reported, these learning projects were usually self-planned (73 percent); professionals, friends, peers, and nonhuman resources accounted for the remainder. The most common reason why a person chose self-planning was reported by McCatty (1975) as the desire to learn particular things, not to survey a field. McCatty also reported that the selection of private and group instruction for a learning project was based on the learner's perception of a teacher's capabilities. However, Penland (1979) reported that the most important reason why adults prefer to learn on their own, instead of in a class, is a positive desire to have more control over the learning process.

As might be expected, the setting of objectives has been found to be the most common problem for the autonomous learner. Knowles (1975) responded by suggesting that the learner develop a learning plan. Such a plan, in the form of an individual learning contract with oneself, begins with specific objectives and includes possible resources along with a means for evaluating the learning project.

The use of specific methods and techniques will vary with the learner's experience and motivation. If the learner opts to take a course as the means for completing a learning project, then the use of group methods and techniques and the degree of structure will be governed by the mode of instruction, institutional or shared membership. However, if the learning is independent of group learning, then the methods and techniques used in the learning project can range from self-directed reading to learning through the use of highly structured independent study methods, such as correspondence courses or programmed learning packages.

Evaluation under the individual mode varies from informal feedback on a learning project to attainment of specific objectives by way of a personal learning contract.

Summary

The goal of fostering participation in the learning process must begin with an understanding of the unique characteristics of adult learners. The learning process has been examined here in the context of Blaney's (1974) comprehensive model of curriculum formation, which distinguishes the institutional mode, the shared membership mode, and the individual mode.

Under the institutional mode, learning is based on highly structured teacher directives that focus on content-centered continuing education. Although the learning process begins with what is to be taught and who is to teach it, some learner participation is possible if the teacher understands the unique characteristics of the adult learner and brings them into play when using methods and techniques.

The shared membership mode may involve either problem-centered or learner-centered continuing education. In both cases, the teacher fosters participation by establishing a positive, accepting group climate for collaborative planning, delivery, and evaluation of appropriate learning activities.

The individual mode places the responsibility for learning squarely on the adult learner through self-directed learning projects. As Tough (1971, p. 170) optimistically wrote concerning this mode of learner participation, "the adult learner of the future will be highly competent in deciding what to learn and planning and arranging his own learning. He will successfully diagnose and solve almost any problem or difficulty that arises. He will obtain help competently and quickly, but only when necessary."

References

Adams, E. *Unearthing Seeds of Fire: The Idea of Highlander.* Winston Salem, N.C.: John F. Blair, 1975.

Apps, J. W. *Toward a Working Philosophy of Adult Education.* Syracuse, N.Y.: Publications in Continuing Education, 1973.

Blaney, J. "Program Development and Curricular Authority." In J. Blaney, I. Housego, and G. McIntosh (Eds.), *Program Development in Education.* Vancouver: University of British Columbia, 1974.

Conti, G. J. *Does Teaching Style Make a Difference?* College Station: Texas A&M University, 1983.

Cross, K. P. *Adults as Learners: Increasing Participation and Facilitating Learning.* San Francisco: Jossey-Bass, 1981.

Dubin, S. S., and Okun, M. "Implications of Learning Theories for Adult Instruction." *Adult Education,* 1973, *24* (1), 3–19.

Kidd, J. R. *How Adults Learn.* New York: Association Press, 1973.

Knowles, M. S. *Self-Directed Learning: A Guide for Learners and Teachers.* New York: Association Press, 1975.

Knowles, M. S. *The Modern Practice of Adult Education from Pedagogy to Andragogy.* Chicago: Follett, 1980.

Lindeman, E. *The Meaning of Adult Education.* Montreal: Harvest House, 1961. (Originally published 1926).

Little, D. "Adult Learning and Education: A Concept Analysis." In P. M. Cunningham (Ed.), *Yearbook of Adult and Continuing Education,* Chicago: Marquis Academic Media, 1979.

McCatty, C. "Patterns of Learning Projects Among Professional Men." *Alberta Journal of Educational Research,* 1975, *21,* 116–129.

McClusky, H. Y. "An Approach to a Differential Psychology." In M. Knowles (Ed.), *The Adult Learner: A Neglected Species.* Houston: Gulf, 1973.

Penland, P. "Self-Initiated Learning." *Adult Education,* 1979, *29* (3), 170–179.

Popham, W. J. *The Teacher Empiricist: A Curriculum and Study Supplement.* Los Angeles: Aegeus Press, 1965.

Rogers, C. R. *Freedom to Learn.* Columbus, Ohio: Merrill, 1969.

Smith, R. M. *Learning How to Learn: Applied Theory for Adults.* Chicago: Follett, 1982.

Tough, A. *The Adult's Learning Projects: A Fresh Approach to Theory and Practice in Adult Learning.* Toronto: Ontario Institute for Studies in Education, 1971.

Tough, A. "Major Learning Efforts: Recent Research and Future Directions." *Adult Education,* 1978, *28* (4), 250–263.

Zahn, J. "Differences Between Adults and Youths Affecting Learning." *Adult Education,* 1967, *17* (2), 67–77.

John A. Niemi is professor of adult education at Northern Illinois University. He was a Fulbright professor of adult education at the University of Helsinki. He is chair-elect of the Commission of Professors of Adult Education.

Whether the goal of the continuing educator is increased student achievement and satisfaction or learner empowerment, involving the adult in educational planning is crucial.

The Adult's Role in Educational Planning

Sandra H. Rosenblum

Although we live in a society where the words of acknowledged experts are often received as gospel, our fascination with authority shows some indication of waning. Scientists and industrialists, politicians and educators have been found to be as fallible as other human beings, and their expert information is greeted with skepticism by some and with open defiance by others.

In significant areas of our lives, such as the classroom and the workplace, the process of unilateral planning and decision making by experts is already being restructured to ensure that fewer individuals are left with small, meaningless areas of discretion. It is considered axiomatic that people respond in more positive ways to their roles in society as they share in the opportunity to participate in matters vital to them (Bluestone, 1974). Participative planning is based on the premise that individuals accomplish more if they feel that they are shaping their own destinies (Humphrey, 1974).

The purpose of this chapter is to examine the reasons why adult participation in planning is viewed as such an essential process, to review the research findings on involvement in planning, and to discuss the implications for continuing educators of varying orientations of incorporating participative planning strategies into their own practice.

S. H. Rosenblum (Ed.). *Involving Adults in the Educational Process.* New Directions for Continuing Education, no. 26. San Francisco: Jossey-Bass, June 1985.

Social Psychologists and Sociologists View Participation

Both social psychologists and sociologists have conducted in-depth analyses of participation as it pertains to social action. These studies are extremely relevant to continuing education, because they focus on small groups in a social milieu.

Of the many generalizations growing out of the experimental study of groups, one of the most broadly and firmly established is that the members of a group tend to be more satisfied if they have at least some feeling of participation in its decisions. Beal and others (1962, p. 89) found that sociological research seems to indicate that, "even when an individual's ideas do not agree with the final group decision, he is much happier when he has had an opportunity to participate and express himself in the decision-making process."

Riecken and Homans (1954, p. 811) point to an individual's feeling of being left out of the decision-making process as one of the major reasons for low member satisfaction in a group situation. The group member sees himself or herself as an individual "who is being told what to do, without being asked what he wants to do, and without being informed of what is going on." It certainly follows, then, that the imposition of a plan on members of a group from without can lead to dissatisfaction.

Gains in efficiency can also be an important by-product of enlisting a group's participation. Thibaut and Kelley (1959, p. 272) state that, "if general participation in developing and planning a means to personal and group goals heightens understanding of it and a commitment to it, the group problem-solving process may be more economical in the long run than one that begins with the most expert thought and advice."

Referring specifically to the classroom situation, Luft (1970, p. 87) asserts that a class as a group may have a need to participate with the teacher in setting goals and establishing structures, in developing its norms for behavior, and in finding its channels and means of communication. He stresses that, when a group of students develops norms such that new perceptions and new questions are part of the group's own purpose or goals, then the process of learning will have been significantly strengthened for each individual learner.

This body of literature shows alternative ways of managing groups and indicates the enormous potential that exists when a participatory approach is enlisted. It suggests that, when an educational activity is proposed by the group, students will have more of a stake individually and collectively in its success than they will if it is imposed by the instructor. Moreover, such evidence is not confined to social groups outside the work situation. These general findings have been substantiated by widespread observations and study of group relationships in the workplace as well.

Workplace Research

Research in the workplace regarding employee participation in planning and decision making indicates that participatory approaches are not only possible but usually superior to traditional authoritarian methods. After examining studies in communist, socialist, and capitalist societies, Tannenbaum and Cooke (1978) report widespread approval of participatory decision making. In an extensive investigation of 3,641 managers in fourteen countries, Haire and others (1966) found that in all cultures studied democratic methods of leadership were viewed most favorably.

Coch and French (1948) conducted a classic study of participation in planning. They interviewed factory workers who had been transferred to new jobs. The results of the study showed clearly that participation in the orientation, retraining, and planning programs helped the workers to adjust to the change in jobs and to improve their production with virtually no turnover or grievances.

The dramatic results of the Coch and French experiment were not repeated, however, when French and others (1960) replicated the study in a Norwegian factory. Interestingly, they found that participation in planning was important only to the extent that the decisions to be made were important to the participants. According to the authors (p. 5), "if the decision is of no importance to the participant and if he does not want to influence it, his participation will make no difference, for it will not provide a means to satisfy his needs." This experiment raises provocative questions for the study of participation. It indicates that the act of participation can be a meaningless exercise if participants view the issues to be discussed and acted upon as insignificant or irrelevant. Involvement in selection of the issues to be addressed enables the participants to choose the areas that are relevant to them and that they would like to influence through their participation.

Participation in Decision Making. Four other studies (Indik and others, 1961; Lawler and Hackman, 1969; Morse and Reimer, 1956; Wickert, 1951) stress the significance of involvement in decision making in the workplace. In all four studies, improvement was observed in employee absenteeism, productivity, or morale as a result of increased participation by workers in decision making.

However, Jacobs (1971) proposed that a leader does not need to use participatory methods in all cases. When time pressures are great and when the leader has all the information he or she needs, participation "might even be perceived as wasteful and therefore resented" (p. 82).

Rather than whether workers should be included in planning and decision making or not, a more appropriate question in the workplace seems to be, Under what circumstances is participation in planning and decision making most appropriate and effective? Bridges (1967) suggests that including individuals in the making of decisions located within their zone of acceptance (a range of behavior where workers are ready to accept decisions made by supervisors) is much less effective than including them in the making of decisions clearly outside their zone of acceptance.

Relevance and Expertise. In an effort to determine under what conditions workers want to be included in the decision-making process, Hoy and Miskel (1978) proposed two tests to identify issues that clearly fall within the zone of acceptance: the test of relevance and the test of expertise. The authors maintain that the test of relevance is imbedded in the question, Do the employees have a high personal stake in the decision? A high personal stake usually points to a high interest in participation. If employees have no personal stake in the decision, they will probably have little interest in participation.

The test of expertise focuses on the extent to which individuals feel qualified to make useful contributions to the problem-solving process. When individuals are asked to participate in decision making outside their experience and competence, they are not interested.

Hoy and Miskel (1978) conclude that, if employees have a personal stake in the decision (high relevance) and have the knowledge to make a contribution (high expertise), then the decision clearly falls outside the zone of acceptance, and employees should be included in the process of decision making. However, if the issue is not relevant and if it falls outside their sphere of competence, then the decision clearly falls within the zone of aceptance, and involvement should be avoided.

Change in Social Relations. Although the findings of workplace research are not totally conclusive, they suggest that new standards, methods of operation, and decisions are more rapidly accepted when the individual participates in determining them than when they are "introduced by fiat or with exhortations and assurances" (Kelley and Thibaut, 1954, p. 756). The democratic management model is not just another management technique but rather the expression of a new perspective on social relations which posits that people want to be associated with the making of decisions that affect them (Schregle, 1976).

Views of Continuing Educators

The concept of including the adult learner in the planning of educational activities is not at all new in the literature on continuing education. In fact, one discovers that writers have repeatedly declared that one of the cardinal principles of sound adult education is to ensure the participation of students in the planning as well as in the execution of programs (Thomas, 1964). Kotinsky (1933, p. 277) stated that, the more the adult educator does alone, the less significant the outcome becomes: "There is no stage so educative for [adult students], so charged with value for them, as that which they have themselves made, suited to their needs and desires, and marred by their own deficiencies to overcome."

The full-participation view of continuing education supports the idea that planning for adult learners should not be done unilaterally by the teacher-expert. The assumption of the responsibility for planning by the authority is "so glaringly in conflict with the adult's need to be self-directing that a cardinal principle of andragogy and, in fact, all humanistic and education theory is that a mechanism must be provided for involving all the parties concerned in the planning of the educational enterprise" (Knowles, 1978, p. 115). Bergevin (1967) maintains that participants will become actively concerned and involved when they are asked to share the planning and management with fellow learners. The problem, Bergevin (1967, p. 154) contends is that, "too often we are not given any opportunity to assume responsibilities, and therefore we can't very well learn to assume them." According to Boyle (1958), "everyone who is affected by a policy decision or a program should share in its making."

Views on Planning. According to Bergevin and others (1963), the aim of adult education is to help us to change, to acquire new knowledge and information in order to help us mature. Although these authors see careful planning as significant in preparing conditions for change, they contend that much of continuing education planning is in actual practice haphazard.

A major problem facing continuing education is that knowledge about program planning is limited. Verner (1963) believes that a combination of the deficiency in knowledge regarding planning and the weight of tradition tends to produce adult education programs that focus on subject matter rather than on the learning objectives and developmental tasks of the adult learner. Miles (1964) is also concerned about the effects of tradition on adult learning. He blames the resistance and anxiety that adult students often experience on childhood education. He maintains (pp. 461–462) that "such phenomena are mute testimony to a lack of childhood practice in cooperative planning of learning experiences."

Benne (1955) notes the importance of involving students in planning and lists three significant benefits of the process: First, decisions and actions are enriched by the knowledge, insight, and imagination of many different people. Second, the plans made and the actions taken are more likely to meet all the varied needs of the people involved, and they fit the unique features of the situation. Third, because each person plays a part in making decisions, he or she is more concerned and interested; people who are actively involved do not need to be sold.

Assessing Needs. Many continuing educators view collaborative diagnosis of the needs of participants as the first step in planning a successful program. It is not enough, according to McKenzie (1973, p. 4) for the instructor to determine the learner's needs. The participants must recognize that the needs exist: "Unless this condition is brought about, adult learning opportunities based upon the results of the diagnosis will not be meaningful to the client." The consensus of continuing education practitioners is that significant learning will take place when the topics that are being discussed are problems for the learner. The learning experience should develop from the level of participants' understanding, background, and experience, and it should be based on the needs and interests that they themselves feel or that they can be assisted to recognize (Boyle, 1958; Gibb, 1960; London, 1960).

Continuing educators often view the instructor as a valuable resource for assisting participants to recognize their needs. Knowles (1967) states that skilled educators are adept in helping participants to diagnose their own needs for learning, while Bergevin and others (1963) suggest that guidance and training can make adults capable of sharing in the planning of their activities.

Setting Goals. It is generally agreed that determination of objectives for a program is the second step in the program-planning process. Objectives help in framing the learning activity into a logical sequence, in selecting resources and techniques, and in determining topics to be included or emphasized.

Bergevin (1967, pp. 136) suggests that, when a group is involved in goal setting, the goals are "often more realistic than when goals are established by the administrator alone, realistic, that is, in satisfying the particular needs of the learners." He lists seven advantages of realistic goal setting: First, clear-cut, realistic goals that can be achieved give learners a sense of accomplishment that is vital in motivating them to continue to pursue the program that they are engaged in and to participate in other programs. Second, as learners help to chart the course of a learning program, they learn to assume responsibility by taking responsibility. Third, participants learn to express their own needs, recognize the needs of fellow learners, and establish a goal that reconciles these possibly different needs. Fourth, participants can learn to relate and work together on a common task. Fifth, a person who is concerned is easier to motivate; when he or she sets the goal, he or she is involved. Sixth, goals tell us where we are going. Seventh, when a goal is realistically set by all members, it is less troublesome to adjust later.

The general consensus of continuing educators is that goals must be set by those included in the program. As a means of making certain that the objectives arrived at take the needs and problems of the participants into account, adult learners should be able to influence the learning goals set for their activity.

Determining Format. The third step in program planning is to decide on the format to be followed. Although there is little research on the subject of format, most adult educators support the view that adult learners should be involved in determining the learning format as well as the other aspects of the program. Sheats and others (1953, p. 322) postulate that it is "probably equally true that democratic procedures demand not only that groups shall determine their goals, but they should also have a major responsibility in determining the methods to be used in reaching them."

It becomes abundantly clear that learner participation in program planning is widely held to be a sound continuing education procedure. The literature attests that this point of view is universal among theorists and practitioners. However, this view is based primarily on experience and intuition, since there is little research to support it.

Educational Research on Participative Planning

Few studies have addressed the issue of participation in program planning from an educational perspective (Rosenblum and Darkenwald, 1983). Both McLoughlin (1971) and Cole and Glass (1977) used similar designs to evaluate the effects of participation on achievement and attitude. In both studies, the experimental groups participated in planning their own programs, while the control groups had no planning input but completed the course as formulated by the experimental groups. Although both studies found that adults who participated in program planning had more positive attitudes toward the course than those who did not, they reached conflicting conclusions about achievement.

McLoughlin (1971) found that participation in planning had no effect on achievement, while Cole and Glass (1977) reported higher achievement levels for the adults who planned their own course. Unfortunately, both studies were methodologically flawed.

Contradictory Conclusions. Three other studies found conflicting results. Using the nominal group technique as a method of ensuring participatory planning, Vedros (1979) found higher achievement but no difference in satisfaction for experimental group subjects who planned their own courses. Weldon (1966) reported greater satisfaction among participants who were involved in planning their own conference than among those who had no input. However, Semberger (1972) found that participation in the planning and implementation of the conference program made no difference as far as participants' satisfaction was concerned.

A Study of Supervisory Classes. My own research into participation in program planning was designed to avoid the methodological problems that marred earlier investigations. Two field experiments were conducted with supervisory employees of a large psychiatric hospital. Phase-one subjects were twenty-eight nursing supervisors who volunteered to participate in a course on supervision for nurses. Phase-two subjects were twenty-six support service supervisors employed in food service, purchasing, and other nonmedical areas. In each phase, participants were assigned at random to experimental and control classes in supervision.

To maximize experimental control, the number of class hours, the room, the time of day, the instructor, and even the refreshments were the same for both experimental and control groups. The class sessions were scheduled weekly for one-and-a-half-hour sessions during work hours for six consecutive weeks.

During the first class session with the experimental groups, the nominal group technique (NGT) was used to ensure group participation in planning the course. The NGT is a structured process for identifying and prioritizing needs or problems (Delbecq and Van de Ven, 1971). Each experimental group identified and prioritized its needs and concerns; then, using a worksheet designed by Knowles (1970), the group decided on four objectives, one for each of the four instructional sessions of the course. The experimental groups also selected the learning formats. The experimental classes participated in an initial planning session, four instructional sessions, and a final examination and evaluation session.

The control groups were not asked to participate in course planning during the first session. Instead of enlisting their participation in planning during the first session, the instructor informed them of the plans that had been developed for the course. The list of needs, the course objectives, and the format to be followed that the respective experimental groups had decided on were presented to the control groups as a course plan arrived at by the instructor. Like the experimental groups, the control groups met six times. At the first session, they were told about the course plans. They met for four instructional sessions identical to those of the experimental groups and for a final test and evaluation meeting.

The results of the two experiments were virtually identical, despite the fact that they were conducted with very different populations. In both experiments, no differences were found in either achievement or satisfaction levels between the groups that had participated in planning the course and the groups that had not.

Interpreting the Results. Did this study indicate that continuing educators do not need to involve participants in the planning process? Probably not. A close look must be taken at the manner in which the courses were developed, at those who developed them, and at the students who participated in the experiment. Although the control groups did not participate at all in the planning of the course, the planning was conducted by their colleagues—coworkers with identical job titles who faced the same daily problems. When the problem list that had been formulated at the planning session of the experimental groups was presented to each control group, the problems enumerated were greeted with sounds of affirmation, nods of approval, and total recognition and acceptance. Similar reactions were forthcoming when the objectives for the class were announced. Because the experimental and control groups were as similar as possible in every way, it seems likely that the plans for the courses addressed the needs of the participants in the control groups as effectively as they did the needs of participants in the experimental groups.

Addressing Participant Concerns. The findings could be interpreted as indicating that, when a course is developed by a group of individuals that is very similar in its characteristics and needs to a second group, the factor of nonparticipation in planning the course does not affect either achievement or satisfaction. The critical element does not appear to be direct involvement in course planning but that the course addresses the concerns of participants. The implication is that, if an instructor is planning to offer a course to a number of similar groups, it may be unnecessary to repeat the planning process with each group individually.

Although achievement and satisfaction were not affected by

participation in planning, significant differences between the groups were observed by the instructor and an impartial observer. Whereas the control group was pessimistic about effecting any meaningful improvement in their jobs as supervisors, the experimental group exhibited a much more positive attitude toward the possibility of change. It is possible that the experience of participating in the program-planning process, of being asked to articulate problems of concern, gave the experimental group a sense of empowerment about making changes in their job situations. Moreover, the members of the nurses' experimental group appeared to be more involved than the control group in class discussions; they participated more, and they tended to direct their discussion more to one another than to the instructor.

A significant footnote to the experiment was that, as an outgrowth of the class, members of the nurses' group who had been involved in planning the course formed an organization at the hospital to discuss and take collective action on common problems and concerns.

Conclusion

As we attempt to arrive at conclusions regarding the role of adults in program planning, it becomes clear that the outcomes we desire from our educational programs have a profound bearing on how we view planning. For the continuing educator working in a traditional setting where the major concerns are student achievement and student satisfaction, the findings of research, albeit somewhat contradictory, point to the conclusion that direct participation in planning may not alter student test scores or attitudes about the course in significant ways. What seems to be more important to participants than direct involvement in planning is that the course addresses their needs and concerns. Learners seem to be as pleased with and to do as well in a course created by proxy planners who have comparable needs and concerns as they are when they take part in the planning themselves.

The question remains, How would learners react to and achieve in a course designed not with input from themselves or from peers but by a consultant? It is apparent that much more research is needed before we can make firm assertions about the effects of participation in planning on achievement and satisfaction.

Empowering Learners. If the concern of the continuing educator is not only to maximize satisfaction and achievement but to structure an environment that makes empowerment of the learner the major goal, the role of involvement in planning will be addressed differently, and different research questions will be posed. Since empowerment education focuses on the learner's becoming critically conscious of power relationships, such learning demands that the power over what one learns no longer be the exclusive domain of the instructor (Cunningham, 1983). According to this approach, the learning group, including the instructor, negotiates procedures, curriculum, objectives, learning methods, and the means by which learning is evaluated. "The term *negotiation* implies a sharing of power by all members of the group rather than an abrogation of power by the tutor" (Nottingham Andragogy Group, 1983, p. 83.) The questions then become these: First, how does participation in planning change the power relationships between learner and instructor? Second, how does involvement in planning give learners an opportunity to gain control over their own thinking and learning?

Educator-Learner Partnership. Although it may be extremely difficult to ascertain the ways in which becoming a partner in program planning alters consciousness in the individual learner, an evaluation of group processes within the learning situation should begin to provide us with answers to the three questions just asked. Researchers should find it possible to observe and record how the continuing educator begins to share power with the group and how the group takes on responsibility. It should also be possible to observe and evaluate how learners become involved in decision making regarding what they learn and how they learn it (Nottingham Andragogy Group, 1983).

Continuing educators can differ widely in the outcomes that they desire for students. For some, the major concerns may be achievement and satisfaction. For others, the issue of learner empowerment is of paramount importance. Nevertheless, involving the adult learner in educational planning is an extremely significant issue for us all, and it deserves substantially more thought and research than it has yet received.

References

Beal, G. M., Bohlen, J. M., and Raudabaugh, N. J. *Leadership and Dynamic Group Action.* Ames: Iowa State University Press, 1962.

Benne, K. *Planning Better Programs.* Leadership Pamphlet 2. Chicago: Adult Education Association of the U.S.A., 1955.

Bergevin, P. *A Philosophy for Adult Education.* New York: Seabury Press, 1967.

Bergevin, P., Morris, D., and Smith, R. M. *Adult Education Procedures.* Greenwich, Conn.: Seabury Press, 1963.

Bluestone, I. "Worker Participation in Decision Making." In R. P. Fairfield (Ed.), *Humanizing the Workplace.* Buffalo, N.Y.: Prometheus Books, 1974.

Boyle, P. "Planning with Principles." *Adult Education,* 1958, *8,* 23–24.

Bridges, E. M. "A Model for Shared Decision Making in the School Principalship." *Education Administration Quarterly,* 1967, *3,* 49–61.

Coch, L., and French, J. R. P., Jr. "Overcoming Resistance to Change." *Human Relations,* 1948, *1,* 512–532.

Cole, J., and Glass, J. C. "The Effect of Adult Student Participation in Program Planning on Achievement, Retention, and Attitude." *Adult Education,* 1977, *27,* 75–88.

Cunningham, P. M. "Helping Students Extract Meaning from Experience." In R. M. Smith (Ed.), *Helping Adults Learn How to Learn.* New Directions for Continuing Education, no. 19. San Francisco: Jossey-Bass, 1983.

Delbecq, A. L., and Van de Ven, A. H. "A Group Process Model for Problem Identification and Program Planning." *Journal of Applied Behavioral Sciences,* 1971, *7,* 466–492.

French, J. R. P., Jr., Israel, J., and As, D. "An Experiment on Participation in a Norwegian Factory." *Human Relations,* 1960, *13,* 3–19.

Gibb, J. R. "Learning Theory in Adult Education." In M. S. Knowles (Ed.), *Handbook of Adult Education in the United States.* Chicago: Adult Education Association of the U.S.A., 1960.

Haire, M., Ghiselli, E. F., and Porter, L. W. *Managerial Thinking: An International Study.* New York: Wiley, 1966.

Hoy, W. K., and Miskel, C. G. *Educational Administration.* New York: Random House, 1978.

Humphrey, A. A. "MBO Turned Upside Down." *Management Review,* 1974, *63,* 4–8.

Indik, B. P., Georgopolous, B. S., and Seashore, S. E. "Superior-Subordinate Relationships and Performance." *Personnel Psychology,* 1961, *13,* 357–374.

Jacobs, T. O. *Leadership and Exchange in Formal Organizations.* Alexandria, Va.: Human Resources Research Organization, 1971.

Kelley, H. H., and Thibaut, J. W. "Experimental Studies of Group Problem Solving and Process." In G. Lindsey (Ed.), *Handbook of Social Psychology.* Cambridge: Addison-Wesley, 1954.

Knowles, M. S. "Program Planning for Adults as Learners." *Adult Leadership,* 1967, *15,* 267–268, 278–279.

Knowles, M. S. *The Modern Practice of Adult Education.* New York: Association Press, 1970.

Knowles, M. S. *The Adult Learner: A Neglected Species.* Houston: Gulf, 1978.

Kotinsky, R. *Adult Education and the Social Scene.* New York: Appleton-Century, 1933.

Lawler, E. E., III, and Hackman, J. R. "Impact of Employee Participation in the Development of Pay Incentive Plans." *Journal of Applied Psychology,* 1969, *53,* 467–471.

London, J. "Program Development in Adult Education." In M. S. Knowles (Ed.), *Handbook of Adult Education in the United States.* Chicago: Adult Education Association of the U.S.A., 1960.

Luft, J. *Group Processes.* Palo Alto, Calif.: Mayfield, 1970.

McKenzie, L. *Adult Education: The Diagnostic Procedure.* Bloomington: Indiana University Press, 1973.

McLoughlin, P. D. "Participation of the Adult Learner in Program Planning." Unpublished doctoral dissertation, Western Michigan University, 1971.

Miles, M. B. "The T-Group and the Classroom." In K. D. Benne, L. Bradford, and J. R. Gibb (Eds.), *T-Group Theory and Laboratory Method.* New York: Wiley, 1964.

Morse, N. C., and Reimer, E. "The Experimental Change of a Major Organizational Variable." *Journal of Abnormal and Social Psychology,* 1956, *52,* 120–129.

Nottingham Andragogy Group. "Towards a Developmental Theory of Andragogy." In P. Allman and K. J. Mackie (Eds.), *Adults: Psychological and Educational Perspectives.* Nottingham: University of Nottingham, 1983.

Riecken, H. W., and Homans, G. C. "Psychological Aspects of Social Structure." In G. Lindzey (Ed.), *Handbook of Social Psychology.* Vol. 2. Cambridge, Mass.: Addison-Wesley, 1954.

Rosenblum, S. H. "The Effects of Adult Learner Participation in Course Planning on Achievement and Satisfaction." Unpublished doctoral dissertation, Rutgers University, 1982.

Rosenblum, S. H., and Darkenwald, G. G. "Effects of Adult Learner Participation in Course Planning on Achievement and Satisfaction." *Adult Education Quarterly,* 1983, *33* (3), 147–153.

Schregle, J. "Workers' Participation in Decisions Within Undertakings." *International Labor Review,* 1976, *113,* 1–15.

Semberger, F. M. "Selected Effects of the Participation of Adults in Program Planning." Unpublished doctoral dissertation, Florida State University, 1972.

Sheats, P. A., Jayne, C. D., and Spence, R. B. *Adult Education: The Community Approach.* New York: Dryden Press, 1953.

Tannenbaum, A. S., and Cooke, R. A. "Organizational Control: A Review of Research Employing the Control Graph Method." In C. J. Lammers and D. J. Hickson (Eds.), *Organizations Like and Unlike.* London: Routledge & Kegan Paul, 1978.

Thibaut, J., and Kelley, H. H. *The Social Psychology of Groups.* New York: Wiley, 1959.

Thomas, A. "The Concept of Program in Adult Education." In G. Jensen, A. S. Liverwright, and W. Hallenbeck (Eds.), *Adult Education: Outcomes of an Emerging Field of University Study.* Washington, D. C.: Adult Education Association of the U.S.A., 1964.

Vedros, K. R. "The Nominal Group Technique as a Participatory Planning Method in Adult Education." Unpublished doctoral dissertation, Florida State University, 1979.

Verner, C. "Basic Concepts and Limitations." In J. R. Kidd (Ed.), *Learning and Society.* Toronto: Canadian Association for Adult Education, 1963.

Weldon, E. J. "Program Planning and Program Effectiveness in University Residential Centers." Unpublished doctoral dissertation, University of Chicago, 1966.

Wickert, R. "Turnover and Employees' Feelings of Ego-Involvement in the Day-to-Day Operation of a Company." *Personnel Psychologist,* 1951, *4,* 185–197.

141, 150

Sandra H. Rosenblum is director of education and training at the New York State Psychiatric Institute. She teaches adult education in the Graduate School of Education, Rutgers University.

*The nominal group technique provides a structured process that enables
adults to participate in planning their learning activities.*

Enhancing Participation Through
the Nominal Group Technique

Kathy R. Vedros

As lifelong learning continues to be a necessity for survival in today's
rapidly changing world, the need to provide adults with meaningful
learning experiences is essential. The standard educational methodology of teacher-designed and teacher-directed learning must yield to
educational experiences that tap the skills and interests of adult learners. If educational institutions expect to capture a share of the growing
continuing education market, their course offerings must seek to develop
each adult learner's opportunity for success and achievement to the
fullest.

Few continuing educators will dispute these statements. However, it is often difficult to move from theory to practice. According to
several researchers (Ingalls, 1976; Humphrey, 1974; Thierauf and
others, 1977; Fox, 1981) the void in the development and use of educational programs that involve adults in planning and decision making
may be due in some degree to several important influences: In traditional methods of learning, the teacher is expected to teach, and students are expected to learn. Teachers' ego-involvement precludes their
relinquishing the hierarchical status of formal authority. Existing

S. H. Rosenblum (Ed.). *Involving Adults in the Educational
Process.* New Directions for Continuing Education, no. 26.
San Francisco: Jossey-Bass, June 1985.

methods and techniques for involving learners in planning and decision making are too complex and time-consuming to be feasible in classroom situations. The techniques now available lack the individual participatory style that is essential in adult education. Systemic demands of formal structure, authority, and accountability exert pressures on the curriculum; these pressures make it difficult to change programs so that they meet individual needs. Not all persons desire to participate, either because they lack the ability and knowledge or because they are not sufficiently interested in the process. Finally, program planners may see little value in bringing diverse perspectives to planning and limit participation in order to gain efficiency. With all these resisting influences in mind, I will describe a technique in this chapter that has been shown to be successful in involving adults in educational planning.

Importance of Learner Involvement

The idea of including adult participants in planning their own learning activities is not new in continuing education. A growing body of literature indicates that participatory planning and decision making may be an essential component in the development of effective programs. Knowles (1970) was one of the first to recognize the importance of learner involvement. He believed that a learning situation that includes participatory planning is of prime importance in satisfying the adult learner's need to know. Subsequent research (Douglah, 1970; Ingalls, 1976; Anthony, 1978, Rosenblum and Darkenwald, 1983) continues to reinforce this belief. The researchers conclude that failure to provide learning situations that are congruent with adult self-concepts and that involve adult learners in the planning and decision-making process leads to frustration, conflict, and inability to develop the opportunity for success and achievement to the fullest. Participatory planning and decision making have come to be recognized as essential components in the development of effective continuing education programs.

Participatory Planning and Decision Making

What is meant by participatory planning and decision making? Due to the complexity and variability of adult learning experiences, there is no all-inclusive definition. Knowles (1970) noted that participatory planning is an active process enabling the learner to share in making decisions and in planning activities that directly affect his or her learning. The variety of interpretations that emerged in subsequent research seems to depend on the context in which participation in planning and decision making is used. In general, however, most definitions appear to encompass the precept that participatory planning is an active process involving at least five important dimensions: First, participation in planning is an integral part of the teaching process. Second, participatory pedagogy brings the structure and substance of educational tasks within the direct control of participants. Third, participation is interdisciplinary, and this tendency appears at all levels of education. Fourth, participatory pedagogy redefines roles in the teaching-learning process by recognizing all participants in the process as persons. Fifth, participatory pedagogy puts the control of time and timing into the hands of the learner. Self-direction gives the learner an opportunity to build on previous experience and to time learning activities so that the learner is ready to assimilate them.

Benefits of Learner Participation

Many benefits have been cited as flowing from situations where individuals are permitted to participate in planning and decision making (Thierauf and others, 1977; Anthony, 1978). For example, participants have greater responsibility in the learning experience because they have helped in its creation. Participants may be led to recognize needs that they have not consciously felt. Planning can be as much a learning experience as direct instruction is. Ego-involvement, self-control, and hence higher intrinsic motivation are often facilitated. Heightened feelings of competence and self-esteem are often present, even if no intrinsic rewards are involved. Finally, the number of absences and grievances is reduced.

Douglah (1970) has reported that participants in decision making usually exhibit such outcomes as higher rates of productivity, greater satisfaction, higher morale, more positive attitudes, and fewer symptoms of resistance and conflict. In addition, he suggests that benefits, such as increased morale, higher satisfaction, and greater commitment, can accrue to the educational agency that solicits the active participation of all members in decision making.

In spite of the benefits and the value of including learners in the planning process, participatory involvement is still infrequent. As a possible explanation, Cole and Glass (1977) noted that relatively few studies concretely define how to include the learner in participative strategies. Thus, the lack of practical techniques and definitive examples is a real concern for continuing educators. In search of a participatory process that was both expedient and effective, I encountered the nominal group technique developed by Van de Ven and Delbecq (1974). This technique has proved to conform most closely to the principles of andragogy. Its format increases the opportunity for each individual to make sure that his or her ideas are part of the group's frame of reference; the experience of adults is valued as a rich resource for learning. Group cohesion and interpersonal relationships are stimulated. An important feature of this technique is that it lends itself to the time, logistical, and practical constraints so real in continuing education.

The Nominal Group Technique

The nominal group technique (NGT) is a structured process that seeks to tap the experiences, skills, or feelings of participants. According to its developers, Van de Ven and Delbecq (1974), the primary objective of the NGT is to increase the creative productivity of group action, facilitate group decision making, stimulate the generation of critical ideas, give guidance in the aggregation of individual judgments, and in all these endeavors save human effort and energy and leave participants with a sense of satisfaction. The technique is designed to be a nonthreatening and depersonalized experience that, when implemented, requires approximately one-and-one-half hours. The process allows a variety of individuals, who may or may not know each other, to meet to generate ideas focused on a common interest area. The NGT assumes that almost everyone wishes to participate in program planning, whether it be in business or in education. Yet, the traditional participatory methods based on group interaction present many problems. Comparing the NGT with interacting group process, the developers noted that the NGT stimulates a balanced orientation among group members between task-instrumental and social-emotional concerns. The process forces participants to think and work through the problem.

The NGT Process

The general procedure for the NGT is straightforward. As described by its developers, it has six steps: silent generation of ideas, round-robin recording of ideas, serial discussion for clarification, a preliminary vote, discussion of the preliminary vote, and a final vote. The next six paragraphs discuss each of these steps.

The first step is to present the question to the group in writing. Give participants time to write their ideas down silently and independently. Ask the group to write their ideas in brief statements or phrases.

This step gives participants time to think and prevents aggressive members from dominating and group members from focusing prematurely on single ideas.

Second, after participants have been given time to generate ideas in silence, ask each member of the group in succession to give one idea from his or her list. Record each idea on a flip chart visible to all members. Individuals who have no further items may pass. Explain that discussion of individual items is not appropriate at this stage. This step equalizes input opportunity for all participants and forces the group to explore the problem under consideration fully.

Third, ask group members to explain their reasons for agreement or disagreement and provide an opportunity for participants to express the logic behind their items. The purpose of this step is to clarify the meaning of all items on the list.

At the conclusion of the discussion, distribute five three-by-five-inch cards to each group member. Ask each participant to write the number and title of his or her priority items on the cards. Each item goes on a separate card. Then ask group members to spread the cards before them and rank the items in the following manner: The most serious gets five points, the second most serious four points, the third most serious three points, the fourth most serious two points, and least serious one point. Collect the cards, tally the vote, and record the results on a flip chart in front of the group.

Fifth, ask participants to discuss any new concerns about the items chosen or particular voting patterns. This step gives group members one last opportunity to clarify their positions.

Sixth, ask participants to vote again in light of the foregoing discussion. Tally the votes, and list the items of group concern on the flip pad in rank order.

The NGT in Continuing Education

The steps of the nominal group technique have been presented as a straightforward procedure. How can we apply this technique in continuing education? In a classroom setting, an instructor can use the NGT to identify learner's goals and priorities for a subject to be presented. For example, the NGT could be used in a course entitled Traveling Abroad for the First Time to generate a list of group concerns and interests most relevant to all attending. The instructor would then have a clear idea of what the participants wanted and expected from the course, and he or she could teach accordingly. The NGT could also be used to identify the elements of a problem, especially where there were political, social, or cultural dimensions. An adult community action group could use the NGT to identify major issues of concern related to new zoning laws, local taxes, political candidates, and so on. An instructor could also use the NGT to identify learner interests for additional course offerings and student services.

Conclusion

The NGT has unlimited potential as a process for involving adults in the design of a structure for their learning activities. The simplicity of the technique makes it easy to implement, and it generates learner involvement in the planning process. Continuing educators who use the technique must be flexible enough in their initial planning to incorporate priorities that learners identify in the nominal group process. Only when educators take the time and effort to listen to students and follow through on their needs will continuing education truly be on target.

References

Anthony, W. P. *Participative Management.* Reading, Mass.: Addison-Wesley, 1978.

Cole, J., and Glass, J. C. "The Effect of Adult Student Participation in Program Planning on Achievement, Retention, and Attitude." *Adult Education,* 1977, *27,* 75–88.

Douglah, M. "Some Perspectives on the Phenomenon of Participation." *Adult Education,* 1970, *20* (2), 88–98.

Fox, R. D. "Formal Organizational Structure and Participation in Planning Continuing Professional Education." *Adult Education,* 1981, *31* (4), 209–226.

Humphrey, A. "MBO Turned Upside Down." *Management Review,* 1974, *63* (8), 4–8.

Ingalls, J. D. *Human Energy: The Critical Factor in Individuals and Organizations.* Reading, Mass.: Addison-Wesley, 1976.

Knowles, M. S. *The Modern Practice of Adult Education.* New York: Association Press, 1970.

Rosenblum, S., and Darkenwald, G. G. "Effects of Adult Learner Participation in Course Planning on Achievement and Satisfaction." *Adult Education Quarterly,* 1983, *33* (3), 147–153.

Thierauf, R. J., Klekamp, R. C., and Geeding, D. W. *Management Principles and Practices.* New York: Wiley, 1977.

Van de Ven, A. H., and Delbecq, A. L. *Group Decision-Making Effectiveness.* Kent, Ohio: Kent State University Center for Business and Economic Research Press, 1974.

Kathy R. Vedros has the doctorate degree in adult education from Florida State University.

Literacy programs can be centers of learning for those who reside outside the mainstream of the dominant culture.

Including Educationally Deprived Adults in the Planning of Literacy Programs

Paul J. Ilsley

This chapter explores the various constraints on student involvement in the process of planning adult literacy programs. Despite philosophical links with such popular credos as respect for individuality, the unique learning needs of all students, and even social reform, student involvement becomes increasingly impossible as the field is professionalized. This chapter examines the cultural traits of illiteracy and the traits of continuing education professionals in order to find the limits of our effectiveness.

Numerous continuing educators view the notion of involvement as central to the planning process (Brockett, 1983; Smith, 1982). These theorists recognize that it is difficult to put the concept into practice. Smith (1982) asserts that it requires great imagination to bring the notion of learning how to learn and self-directed learning into practice. Ewert (1982) believes that involving students in the planning process may actually threaten officials and jeopardize jobs unless certain precautions are taken. Darkenwald (1980) argues that, to win approval, effective

S. H. Rosenblum (Ed.). *Involving Adults in the Educational Process.* New Directions for Continuing Education, no. 26. San Francisco: Jossey-Bass, June 1985.

nontraditional practice requires a certain commitment to excellence. The contributions of these writers are useful because they invite us to examine our practice.

Other writers (Cunningham, 1983; Fingeret, 1983; Heaney, 1983; Illich, 1969, 1970, 1973; McKnight, 1976) look at the broad picture and critically examine not only current practice but also the actual goals of literacy programs. These authors assume that there are cultural constraints on literacy programs. As Cunningham (1982, 1983), Heaney (1983), and Illich (1969) inform us, the solution becomes the problem. That is, instructional methodology may hinder student involvement. As proficiency in instructional methodology increases, student involvement may actually decrease. Heaney (1983) goes so far as to say that the middle-class structure of illiteracy programs, public and volunteer alike, precludes the possibility of rooting out systematic inequality. An alternative idea, according to both Heaney (1983) and Cunningham (1982, 1983), is to help groups of people identify their own problems and then seek solutions from continuing educators as the need arises. For Cunningham (1983), literacy is more than reading and numerical skills. If we accept that illiteracy is part of a larger context involving unemployment, poverty, and powerlessness, we may also accept the view that the top priority is to remove these conditions permanently. Fingeret (1983) illuminates the fact that the culture of illiteracy has unique norms, values, and methods of adaptation.

At the outset it should be understood that literacy programs have many accomplishments; many millions of Americans have benefited from them since 1965. Continuing educators are rightfully inspired by the numerous success stories of adults who have achieved great goals with a minimum amount of help. Nevertheless, this chapter argues that most literacy programs are technology based and that as a result they are culturally incongruent with students' experience.

Cultural Characteristics of Adult Literacy Programs

A culture can be defined as a complex whole that includes customary beliefs, material traits, and social norms peculiar to a specific group, occupation, or profession. At least three cultural characteristics relate to effective student involvement: who controls the definition of the problem, the technology, and organizational and professional goals. As cultural traits, these characteristics continually shape and reshape our profession. The uniqueness of the culture of continuing education is evident when we examine the three traits.

Who Defines the Problem? Houle (1980) believes that professions possess cultural functions, including the capacity to solve problems, the use of practical knowledge, and a quest for self-enhancement. The professionalizing occupations are different from other vocations because their leaders seek to encourage and regulate standards of practice based on a profound central mission and an advanced and esoteric body of knowledge. In continuing education, practice centers on the mission of service. One of our hopes as adult educators is that our mission of service will be enhanced as our expertise increases.

Typically, however, increased professionalism means greater power to define the problems of others. The power to define a problem is considerable, because with responsibility to define a problem comes responsibility to find a solution. McKnight (1976) argues that the civil rights movement would have begun much differently had the problem been labeled a "black" problem, not a "white" or "societal" problem. In this sense, the act of labeling directs expectations for solutions. When discrimination can be labeled a "societal" problem, solutions can be sought in a change of custom, law, and mores, not merely in admonishments to the victims.

An analysis of Houle's (1980) queries on professionalism might lead us to conclude that, when people have a need and entrust the finding of a solution to a professional, the need is transformed into a deficiency. As McKnight (1976) puts it, the very meaning of the word *solution* demands that there be a problem. We do not solve needs. We solve problems. Therefore, our professional solutions exist to remedy problems through the application of professional techniques.

The context of adult literacy education is professional. This means that illiterate adults come to us with a need that we use testing techniques to define as a reading or numerical skills problem. With reasoned analysis, we direct solutions to help people individually learn reading skills. In this way, we define the problem as a "student" problem, not as a societal problem. Our technology is simply not meant to solve societal problems. It was invented to help people gain skills. Even when the setting for learning is the group, the success of our applications of the technology for teaching literacy is measured on an individual basis as the degree to which the skill deficiency has been alleviated. To quote McKnight (1976, p. 9) "The tool defines the problem rather than the problem defining the tool." Thus, one limitation on the involvement of students is that the learning process is professionally determined.

Our solutions may include many positive features, such as selflessness, time, talent, and dedication. Certainly, it is not out of malevolence or arrogance that we label people "students" and thereby limit their rights in the decision-making process. Yet, we remove students from the process of deciding what the problem is and instead include them in the definition of the problem. "You don't know how to read; I can teach you" is tantamount to saying "You have a problem; I have the answer" or "You are the problem; I am the answer." Despite our flexibility and understanding that rates of learning and interest areas vary, students are excluded from deciding for themselves either the problems or the context. Their education is done on our terms.

The argument can be raised that students do not always know what they want. How can they be involved in decision making for learning when they do not know what they should know? Of course, not everyone has the ability to solve his or her own problems individually. But there is a profound difference between teaching to eliminate deficiencies and creating conditions that allow others to determine their own problems.

The Technology. Illich (1973) points out that some tools are manipulative, while others are convivial. A tool is said to be manipulative when one needs permission to use it or when one is otherwise obstructed from using it. A tool is convivial when anyone is free to use it or to learn how to use it. Roads, drugs, and lesson plans are examples of manipulative tools, because their legal use lies in the domain of licenses or professional persons. A crowbar, tomato seeds, and a telephone are examples of convivial tools. One typically does not need permission to use them. Of course, some tools are more convivial than others.

The norm in continuing education is not to certify educator expertise, yet we assume that many of our tools are beyond the reasoned capacities of our students. For example, to what avail would it be to teach our students how to diagnose their own needs? For one thing, it appears that students would be working at cross-purposes. For another, we assume that a certain level of expertise beyond students' skills is required. One way of investigating how the tools are manipulated is to examine how we label them. Such terms as *notional-functional* and *adult performance levels* are alien to students and show them that the correct use of our tools is the domain of professionalism.

Our tools are born of our mission of service, but the logic of our technique organizes us professionally. As professionals, we rightfully seek security and status in a competitive society. It is quite understandable, in fact, that continuing educators have sought legitimacy. We also seek to be responsive to the needs of our students. Our cultural norms have developed in such a way that we respect self-directed learning and value a lifelong learning society that charges institutions to help people to realize their potential. Unfortunately, there are contradictions in the cultural values of continuing education. The tools that we use and sometimes label in forbidding ways may promote legitimacy, but they also inhibit student involvement. To cite one example, in adult basic education, we have borrowed heavily from the medical profession, which has legitimacy and status in our society, to find a pathway for our own professional status. Thus, in our learning clinics, not only do we diagnose students, we prescribe individual treatments. Moreover, we monitor the conditions until goals have been reached, at which time students may be terminated (sic).

The main point is that, to a greater or lesser extent, students submit to the logic of our technique. What this means in practical terms is that they lose personal agency to the technician. Teachers in literacy settings become "advocates" for students. In so doing, they administer various assessment and planning techniques and summon materials to fit the situation. Despite attempts to draw student interests to the forefront, advocacy means that students depend on the teacher's expertise and rely on the teacher to suggest the next step. Mystification of tools can become so complete that issues of values and political matters are forced into the subjective, because they are not manageable with our techniques. When we can transform and disguise human aspirations as technological problems, we then can apply technological solutions. However, for human aspirations to be taken seriously, they must find meaning in a technological base. It is therefore rare to find literacy programs that bring tools to bear on situations of poverty and even on poor health and unemployment. It is not that continuing educators are unaware of these problems or that they wish to ignore them. The issue is that, aside from some exemplary programs, our tools fail us.

Organizational and Professional Goals

If we take the long view, continuing education programs are specific forms of management. They are programs that have as an attending responsibility the rationalization of procedure centered on formally articulated goals. To the extent that continuing education programs are formal organizations, the following characteristics apply: First, they have established and fixed jurisdictional areas, not only geographic but also with regard to service areas. While continuing educational programs are not intended to be all things to all people, what they are supposed to achieve is a conscious decision of planners. Second, they are usually part of a larger system of agencies, and to some extent they are governed by hierarchical principles. Within continuing education programs, there is division of labor, which calls for specialization of service. Goal setting is not necessarily within the hierarchical province of all members of continuing education agency, but constraints of service are limited mostly by imagination. Third, management of instruction is based on organized procedures. It is a sign that a program is efficient when procedures for instruction are routinized. Fourth, management of the agency follows general rules and is based on written records. Fifth, training is typically required of employees of continuing education agencies. Training may be a vehicle for innovation, or it may foster the routinization of procedure. Moreover, the job of continuing educator frequently requires the full working capacity of the individual. Doing adult education requires considerable expertise.

The organizational procedures used in continuing education settings are indicative of the bureaucratic nature of organization. As such, the goals of education organizations include efficiency and consistency. To the extent that democratic systems of management interfere with efficiency and consistency in continuing education settings, not only among teachers but especially among students, democracy is often controlled or canceled. The route more often traveled to efficiency is management by hierarchy. If the assertion that continuing education programs are hierarchical more often than not is correct, is it not also true that the goal of student involvement faces organizational obstacles?

According to Weber (1958), bureaucracies face increasing complexity. Although they are designed for efficiency and consistency, those goals can be achieved only through such means as division of labor. It is not necessary, and in some cases it is not possible, for all members to understand the workings of an entire organization. One postulate is that, as an organization becomes increasingly complex, it becomes increasingly difficult for people to understand as a whole. Viewed this way, the notion of student involvement faces serious obstacles in the future. It is logical to conclude that the following course of events will characterize an increasingly complex continuing education organization: First, individual comprehension of the policies and programs of the agency will diminish. Second, motivation to allow students or volunteers to participate in the decision-making process will diminish, especially at the higher levels. Third, student involvement in decision making will decline, and adherence to rationally organized plans of action will become stricter. Fourth, expertise will receive increased recognition, especially with regard to goals and methods of instruction. Fifth, the proportion of the budget spent on controlling curricula through training, hiring practices, certification, and specialization of curriculum construction will increase. Sixth, the alienation between students and professional educators and the perception among those who refuse to join the system that it is degrading will both increase. Seventh, rigidity of service and a narrowing of diversity and innovation will cause flexibility of purpose to decline. Eighth, vulnerability to obsolescence will increase.

McKnight (1976) and Illich (1973) support the contention that professional organizations typically surpass their usefulness because it costs increasingly more to achieve increasingly less. McKnight (1976), describing the "iatrogenic" argument, explains that it is possible for professions not only to become less useful but actually to create the problem they intend to resolve. Thus, courts may "create" injustice and crime, hospitals may "produce" sick people, transportation systems may slow travel, and education programs may "cause" befuddlement and dependency. It offends the mind to consider such possibilities. Illich (1973) uses the metaphor of "watersheds" to describe the phenomenon. Resources of time and money increase disproportionately in relation to the benefits received. As the human and material resources spent on such control mechanisms as personnel processes, screening and diagnosis techniques, and curriculum construction increase, a program becomes less efficient relative to the number of students served. That is when the second watershed is reached. The third watershed is brought on by the inclusion of compulsory services, forced learning, and alienated participants. In such an instance, not only do programs become even more expensive, they may also become social liabilities to students.

Transcending Professionalism: The Renewal of the Adult Literacy Movement

The preceding discussion introduces the possibility that despite our best intentions, student involvement in adult literacy programs is a tentative and typically unsuccessful practice. We have examined three of the many factors that influence the quality of student involvement: who defines the problems, the technology, and the goal of professions and organizations. I hope these themes will challenge continuing educators, especially adult basic educators and adult educators in literacy volunteer settings, to recognize that there are systemic limits to our effectiveness. True involvement of adult learners in the planning process requires a radical departure from current practice, especially in our way of viewing ourselves and the people we serve.

At this juncture, it may prove helpful to describe the type of program that could avoid the problems associated with professionalization and technicism. Would such a program survive long? Our description should include a realistic assessment of the political chances for survival. Taking the three cultural characteristics that distinguish continuing education programs into account, we can imagine a program that truly provides students with the power to define their own problems, that allows free access to and free use of its tools, that exists to promote students' goals, and that avoids unnecessary reductionism of human purposes through flexibility and realizes instead the value and political nature of education.

Certainly, such a program would assess the corresponding roles of students and teachers carefully. It might place the emphasis on collective analysis of situations and day-to-day problems in recognition of the fact that collegial airing of issues and concerns is to be preferred to privatization. The role of teacher is transformed from keeper of the technology into facilitator of dialogue. At the same time, the fact that matters of literacy are inextricably linked to culture is acknowledged. With regard to the powerlessness associated with illiteracy, continuing education programs can be centers for discussion for those who reside outside the mainstream of the dominant culture. Social justice, always a concern for those who lack power, becomes a mission within which the goal of literacy is nested.

Educators who implement empowerment programs of this sort are aware of the risks that they take. Chief among them is whether the program will survive. Ewert (1982) examines four problems associated with involving students in the planning process. Although Ewert describes them in the context of programs in foreign lands, they are applicable to programs in North America, urban and rural alike. First, adult participation in the planning process may result in equating an audience's verbalization of a perceived need with an external promise for a programmatic solution to that need. Second, involvement that has this result may lead to political conflict. Third, pure student involvement is a violation of the traditional roles of both student and teacher. The adjustment to new roles is frustrating. Fourth, models of adult education that advocate student involvement threaten the established social order.

On the one hand, given the problems associated with the ideal environment, we must ask whether programs that involve students in the decision-making process are doomed to extinction. On the other hand, if adult literacy programs continue to impose a content-centered approach on students, with its accompanying middle-class values, student involvement is not likely to be realized to any meaningful extent. When it comes to our profound central mission of service, we can ask two thematic questions: First, can the adult basic education movement be appraised in terms of its contributions toward solving the enormous problems now confronting society? Second, has the movement brought us closer toward reckoning with citizen involvement, social change, and disparities between the haves and the have-nots?

Adult literacy education is a movement that is constantly being renewed. While the movement may be tension filled, fluctuating, and dynamic, it clearly represents more than merely the reduction of illiteracy. Yet, a solution to the problem posed by professionalism has yet to be found. It is clear that, as our vision of the future we desire becomes sharper, so will it become easier to get there. Three observations can help to renew our faith in such a vision. First, adult literacy programs can model the practice of inclusive rather than exclusive practices by moving away from specialization that excludes people from learning and knowing. Second, adult literacy programs can use eclectic methodology and allow subjective experiences to enter into the standard subject matter; they do not continually have to invent supposedly value-free curricula. Third, adult literacy programs can open opportunities for people to participate in the decision-making process by reducing the distinction between teacher and student, expert and client.

Adult literacy programs can expand the definition of literacy to include a more holistic and unified view of human experience. Rather than merely treating problems in reading, we can recognize that literacy in the broad sense takes the whole person and the whole person's life context into account. The irony is that the instructional strategy of individualization, instead of promoting student involvement, actually removes people from their social contexts in an apolitical and value-free way. For relevant learning to occur, we must transcend our culture of professionalism.

References

Bledstein, B. J. *The Culture of Professionalism.* New York: Norton, 1976.

Brockett, R. G. "Self-Directed Learning and the Hard-to-Reach Adult." *Lifelong Learning: The Adult Years,* 1983, *6* (8), 16–18.

Cassera, B. "Needs Assessment for the Educationally Underprivileged." In F. C. Pennington (Ed.), *Assessing Educational Needs of Adults.* New Directions for Continuing Education, no. 7. San Francisco: Jossey-Bass, 1980.

Cunningham, P. M. "Contradictions in the Practice of Nontraditional Continuing Education." In S. B. Merriam (Ed.), *Linking Philosophy and Practice.* New Directions for Continuing Education, no. 15. San Francisco: Jossey-Bass, 1982.

Cunningham, P. M. "Helping Students Extract Meaning from Experience." In R. M. Smith (Ed.), *Helping Adults Learn How to Learn.* New Directions for Continuing Education, no. 19. San Francisco: Jossey-Bass, 1983.

Darkenwald, G. G. "Continuing Education and the Hard-to-Reach Adult." In G. G. Darkenwald and G. A. Larson (Eds.), *Reaching Hard-to-Reach Adults.* New Directions for Continuing Education, no. 8. San Francisco: Jossey-Bass, 1980.

Eberle, A., and Robinson, S. *The Adult Illiterate Speaks Out: Personal Perspectives on Learning to Read and Write.* Washington, D.C.: Office of Educational Research and Improvement, National Institute of Education, 1980.

Ewert, D. M. "Involving Adult Learners in Program Planning." In S. B. Merriam (Ed.), *Linking Philosophy and Practice.* New Directions for Continuing Education, no. 15. San Francisco: Jossey-Bass, 1982.

Fingeret, A. "Common Sense and Book Learning: Culture Clash?" *Lifelong Learning: The Adult Years,* 1983, *6* (8), 22–24.

Heaney, T. W. "Adult Learning and Empowerment: Toward a Theory of Liberatory Education." Unpublished doctoral dissertation, Union Graduate School (Chicago), 1980.

Heaney, T. W. "Illiteracy: Towards a Political Solution." In S. Orem (Ed.), *Proceedings of the Midwest Research Conference.* DeKalb: Northern Illinois University Press, 1983.

Houle, C. O. *Continuing Learning in the Professions.* San Francisco: Jossey-Bass, 1980.

Illich, I. D. *Deschooling Society.* New York: Harper & Row, 1970.

Illich, I. D. *Tools for Conviviality.* New York: Harper & Row, 1973.

McKnight, J. "Professionalized Service and Disabling Help." Paper presented at the first annual symposium on bioethics, Montreal, 1976.

Rosenblum, S. H., and Darkenwald, G. G. "Effects of Adult Learner Participation in Course Planning on Achievement and Satisfaction." *Adult Education Quarterly,* 1983, *33* (3), 147–153.

Sisco, B. "The Undereducated: Myth or Reality?" *Lifelong Learning: The Adult Years,* 1983, *6* (8), 14–15, 24, 26.

Smith, R. M. *Learning How to Learn: Applied Theory for Adults.* Chicago: Follett, 1982.

Weber, M. *The Protestant Ethic and the Spirit of Capitalism.* New York: Scribner's, 1958.

Paul J. Ilsley is assistant professor of adult education at Syracuse University. He has spent eleven years working in adult literacy projects in Maine, Chicago, and Syracuse. Ilsley is coauthor of Recruiting and Training Volunteers *(New York: McGraw-Hill, 1981).*

The challenge of distance education is to open a genuine dialogue that builds up the learner's autonomy.

The Challenge of Distance Education

Michael Law
Linda Sissons

Whether continuing educators work in what is strictly defined as distance education or not, they are affected by the challenge of involving adult learners in independent learning, often in learning that takes place at a physical distance from the teacher. Distance education was defined by Michael Moore (1973, p. 664) as "the family of instructional methods in which the teaching behaviors are executed apart from the learning behaviors." As such it can be seen to cover much more than the orthodox correspondence course. Continuing educators who meet their students for only two or three hours a week are all too familiar with, and sometimes perplexed by, the amount of exploring and processing that characteristically goes on within their students between classes. We have to face that for adult students in part-time learning situations the majority of learning is truly at a distance.

There are other points of relevance. It is no coincidence that distance education and adult education both became focuses of attention and study at around the same time. Both have their roots in the revolutionary shift of theoretical and philosophical emphasis that put the

S. H. Rosenblum (Ed.). *Involving Adults in the Educational Process.* New Directions for Continuing Education, no. 26. San Francisco: Jossey-Bass, June 1985.

learner, not the teacher, at the center of the educational enterprise. Once we accept that learning is not necessarily tied to teaching nor restricted to the years of compulsory education, we come face to face with a raft of related problems and challenges.

This chapter looks at some of these problems and challenges. It looks at them in the context of education at a distance, that is, education where it is overtly acknowledged that the teaching behaviors take place at a distance from the learning behaviors and where "communication between the teacher and the learner must be facilitated by print, electronic, mechanical, or other devices" (Moore, 1973, p. 664). We hope that this chapter will raise issues that are important for "face-to-face" educators as well as for distance educators. In distance education, the educator faces problems of facilitating dialogue, of stimulating autonomy, and of structuring the educational experience in such a way that that learner formulates his or her own questions and objectives and evaluates the value of the evidence collected and the arguments adduced; these all may be seen usefully as extensions of the problems with which face-to-face continuing educators must deal.

It will help to show this if we start by defining distance as a matter not of miles but of degrees of clarity and participation. Thus, the learner can be distant even in face-to-face learning situations if the program's structure is unrevealed, unclear, or not open to negotiation and if there is no built-in opportunity for dialogue with the educator. In contrast, the learner in a distance program who works entirely through the printed or written word, telephone, television, and so forth can enjoy a close and egalitarian relationship with the educator if the program has a clear, negotiable structure and if there are ample opportunities for feedback and dialogue.

The challenge to the distance educator to involve the adult learner has its own pressing dimensions. These dimensions include the personal characteristics of the majority of adult correspondence learners, their presenting motivations for undertaking such study, the instrumental orientation of many providers, the inflexibility that results from the prepackaging of teaching materials, the widespread deference shown by adults to the hi-tech concomitants of learning, and the inevitable time elapsed between initiation and response, with its potential for impairing the learning process.

For the social change educator, there are added problems. In distance education, the learner is usually in isolation. The norm is the individual, whereas genuinely radical education for the dispossessed and the silent begins with and uses social experience. Distance education, where materials are prepared in advance and administered ready-made, can be seen as banking education par excellence — the teacher "deposits" knowledge in the uninvolved recipient — whereas Freire (1981) has taught us that learning and teaching consist of mutual work on a problem by both teacher and learner. Radical education presents a fundamental challenge to the distance tradition.

Distance Education for What?

For a constellation of reasons, both learners and educators tend to regard distance education programs as predominantly instrumental. Many distance programs are oriented toward qualifications. People enroll in them in order to get something else, not for the sake of the programs themselves. Providing institutions exploit this attitude in their advertising. This fact needs to be taken into account, since it has influenced the types of development that have taken place; it also influences the attitudes and expectations of learners and teachers and of what they come to regard as possible and appropriate. Let us look at two underlying factors: the history of distance education and the predominance of technology.

History. Distance learning programs have a dual patrimony; neither parent is especially auspicious. The first is the growth of external degree programs at universities where these have traditionally been an alternative educational strategy, a second-best approach, a necessary concession to geography, individuals' physical health, and the social role responsibilities of adults that prevent them from attending regular classes on campus. As John Belchem (1979) has observed with respect to New Zealand, external degrees have a long but grudging history.

The grudging element is manifest in questions of academic acceptability. Thus, the external student tends to be required to meet the demands of the institution's (or in the case of schooling and technical education, the state's) internal assessment criteria. External students study the same materials, complete the same assignments, and take the same examinations as the internal students do. Not surprisingly, therefore, some studies have found that, all things being equal, external students would prefer to study on campus (Dodds and others, 1981).

Within this context, the role of the distance educator is circumscribed by a traditionally technical task. The challenge is to improve performance and increase retention by developing better resource materials, by harnessing new media, and perhaps by providing off-campus support structures.

The other parent is the commercial world. In countries where education is almost entirely state funded, distance education stands out as an arena for private enterprise. The glossy advertisements for distance programs naturally tend to stress the concrete rewards for undertaking the courses: speaking another language by the time you go on holiday, opening your own business, gaining a vocational qualification, and so forth.

Technology. The instrumentality of distance learning programs also reflects the unequal development of educational technologies. The most noteworthy developments in distance education technologies have been directed to behavioral and cognitive ends. The formulation of behavioral and cognitive objectives has become highly sophisticated. Behavioral objectives are now much more detailed than affective objectives. Bloom and others (1964) discuss how the meaning and substance of affective objectives have been eroded by the increased emphasis on cognitive objectives and speak of the need for this erosion to stop. The development of techniques and technologies permitting a whole response encouraging dialogue or autonomy has lagged very much behind the development of technologies of performance. In their absence, instrumentality becomes a feature of distance programs, where the definition of objectives is an important component. Harris and Holmes (1976, pp. 81–82) have written that "the use of behavioral objectives denies subjectivity in important ways. The complex links between thought and knowledge and action are reduced or objectified. Important educational aims like the development of personal understanding are replaced by trivial behaviors which have been prespecified as being desirable outcomes for other people, with no alternatives permitted. Knowledge is seen as being essentially instrumental, aimed solely at producing end behaviors, just as in technical training. The idea of students being able to develop their own personal praxis as a result of what they have gained no longer features as the major point of education."

Otto Peters (1983) has theorized that distance education is the most industrialized form of education. Hence, its forms are entirely complementary to our industrial and technological age. To illustrate, we can point to the division of labor in the production and teaching of programs, the mechanization of the teaching process, the economies of scale, and, by implication, the instrumentality of the programs themselves.

Educator and Learner in Distance Education

Educators and learners both occupy a contradictory place in distance education. A widely advertised and widely felt rationale for distance learning is the freedom that it gives to participants; "in your own time," "from the comfort of your own armchair" are real attractions for very many. For the educator as well, there is freedom to correspond with and to mark and return work to learners in one's own free time.

But, participants in the process are subject to heavy constraints from prepackaged materials, whether they teach or learn; these materials are sometimes prepared by the individual tutor, sometimes by an institution. The experience of thousands in the United Kingdom's Open University has been that it is the "course team," the writers of programs, who produce the insights and engage in learning and discovery, not the teachers or the learners. As Davison (1975, p. 24) writes, "the people who experience exciting and immensely demanding learning tasks are the course teams. They are acquiring and organizing knowledge, evaluating and selecting materials, designing and presenting programs and activities. The student receives what appears to be a polished product from this process; he has to learn from material that has been agonized over by . . . many others. In reality, the home-based learner *receives* at home; he *thinks* in markets, offices, workshops, pews, angling clubs."

This perspective is supported from the evidence of students' own views. Holmberg (1981, p. 24) summarized students' reasons for taking distance courses and concluded that "many adults prefer distance study to other forms of learning because they feel it makes them more independent. This is undoubtedly (in most cases) a reality as far as timing is concerned. The question is whether distance education is or can become a method for acquiring knowledge and skills on conditions decided on by students and thus be a method suitable for autonomous students." The challenge to both learners and educators is to carve out some room for maneuver, room in which they can make their own impression on what is being taught and learned.

The Educator. "In traditional education a teacher teaches. In distance education an institution teaches" (Keegan, 1983, p. 13). Keegan goes on to describe how the personal aspects of teaching are filtered out as a result of this emphasis. Harris and Holmes (1976, p. 83) see distance teaching — "the accumulation of expert knowledge at the center and its rational dispersal to ignorant students on the periphery" — as the triumph of Freire's banking theory of education, especially if we consider the programs produced by large institutions, such as the Open University in the United Kingdom. However, the principles remain operative even when the educator prepares his or her own program. The problems of being unable to control for the response of the learner, to respond at opportune moments so as to provide feedback and insight, and to open oneself to challenge a question even while teaching — these are problems that emphasize the risks of banking.

The Student. There are two traditional archetypes of the distance learner: first, the brilliant loner; second, the disadvantaged, older, less financially prosperous learner. These archetypes need to be examined more closely.

Richardson (1981) looked at some of the evidence indicating that different types of learners profit from different instructional techniques. He centered on two stereotypic adult education client groups, the SAVY adult (Schooled, Active Verbal, and Younger) and the ONUS adult (Older, Not verbal, Unschooled, and Sedentary). The members of these two groups are seen more accurately as at the two ends of a continuum. Following Cross (1981) and others, she suggested that the SAVY adults have personal characteristics — high academic self-concept, active minds, and so forth — that militate in favor of their taking advantage of distance education opportunities and of succeeding in them because of their personal qualities — self-direction, self-confidence, and so forth. In contrast, ONUS individuals are not only less likely to enroll but also more likely to drop out (Anderson and Darkenwald, 1979). Richardson (1981) called for differentiated instructional techniques. She argued that "higher-load" methods — methods that require much more student activity, discovery-oriented, nondirective, unstructured, open-ended, unguided approaches — suit the SAVY learner. ONUS learners require much more highly organized programming, shorter sequences, rapid and accurate feedback, and many directive instructions.

Evidence from a range of countries suggests that motivation is linked at least as much to the way in which the learning opportunities are presented as it is to the characteristics of learners as individuals. When more work has been done on the techniques of reading and learning, practitioners will be better able to assess motivation. Keegan (1983, p. 14) pointed out that "the distance system gives a radical new meaning to the concept of the independence of the adult learner. . . . Questions of motivation and skill acquisition, of a specifically different kind to those required in distance education, need to be tackled to combat the phenomena of nonstarters and dropouts that have been a feature of this type of education throughout the last one hundred years." Elsewhere, Keegan (1983, p. 29) noted that "the ideal in distance education is not necessarily independence but, as John S. Daniel wrote, 'interaction and independence: getting the mixture right.'"

However, it remains a fact that, for the majority of adult distance learners today, their motivation is associated with second-chance considerations. Moreover, the average age tends to be higher than that of students in full-time face-to-face education. Higher age and comparatively less formal education mean a likelihood of less literacy, less confidence. Yet, distance education appears in theory to be more appropriately associated with high literacy and independence from support. Thus, much attention needs to be given to prestudy aspects, such as pre-entry counseling, preparatory and bridging courses, study skills training, and the like. The nature of introductory material needs to be considered very carefully. It is to the concrete aspects of the distance learning experience that we now turn.

Techniques

This discussion centers on a concern for involving the adult learners in distance education. This section on techniques will therefore concentrate on techniques that provide effective structure and dialogue between learner and educator.

Program Preparation. The writers of distance programs and organizations contemplating the production of such programs need to look closely at a range of considerations in order to define their objectives. John A. Baath (1983) has compiled a simple but fairly comprehensive checklist of factors that need to be considered:

- The budget for the course
- The type of course (including its purpose, whether for qualification or hobby)
- The type of distance education (written only, or including other media)
- The nature of the subject (for example, proficiency or orientation)
- The target groups (such characteristics as age and educational background).

The physical presentation of the written material is crucial in inviting participation and dialogue. Written presentation as we normally see it in textbooks has a logic of its own that can quickly become a tyranny if the reader is not encouraged to respond and provided with space for his or her own contributions.

Holmberg (1983) summarizes the available evidence on text elaboration as part of comprehension or learning and on the importance of internalized conversation as one way in which text elaboration proceeds. Conversation requires a number of favorable circumstances: It takes place between two or a few more persons of roughly similar status. It involves more or less equality of input and responsibility. It is comparatively flexible, and it can be fairly free-ranging, although it is centered on a theme. Contributions alternate regularly; it is not all one-way.

Conversation has an element of personal revelation. Finally, it is idiomatic and low-key. Holmberg's term *guided didactic conversation* nicely encapsulates the mix of formality and informality, independence and dependence that characterizes the educational exchange.

In a print medium, the challenge of creating an impression of conversation, even before we start to create the reality of dialogue, is considerable. Two aspects seem to us to be vital. One is the physical positioning of breaks, attention-getters, encouragements to do one's own thinking or searching. Marginal symbols, white areas, a line across the page, and a piece of card supplied to physically stimulate a pause in reading all need to be used, but for genuine reasons and only to encourage, not to force a response. The extreme structuring of programmed learning turns the learner into something more like an experimental animal thumbing urgently through the text than a fellow learner.

The second aspect that we regard as important in admitting the learner into the dialogue involves granting status to the student's written word vis-à-vis the educator's printed word. This status may be symbolic, but it is no less important for that. Correspondence texts can be structured so that input can alternate between educator and student or so that it can be simultaneous (via margins). Or, the text can be in a ring binder format, so that the student can interleave it with his or her notes.

For educators—the vast majority—who have been trained along traditional lines, the model is the book. However, for effective distance learning, we may need to think of other print models, such as loose-leaf notebooks, logbooks, diaries, and grids—models that put the power into the hands of the user. Educators often think of the physical aspects of presentation as secondary, yet they are subtly very influential.

The next aspect of presentation relates to how distance learning can encourage autonomy in the student's approach to an area of learning. Learning that is more than simply the sharing of banked knowledge involves such activities as asking questions, formulating hypotheses, collecting and evaluating evidence, and organizing one's own learning. Can distance learning programs encourage these activities? We believe that they can. Project-based programs are widely used in face-to-face learning. Their principles can be adapted to the distance learning situation, although there are comparatively few models, and presentational techniques have yet to be developed. The useful techniques are likely to include grids (questions versus resources), conceptual diagrams, storage and retrieval systems, and progress reports. Much more work needs to be done in order to structure the methods of formulating questions and of finding and evaluating evidence. It is in these areas that structure and dialogue are essential.

Dialogue Systems. Dialogue requires two real people. In distance learning, the dialogue is more often than not between one person (the student) and a computer, an institution, or a tutor instructed to act as much like an institution or a computer as possible. Much has been written about support systems. We prefer to call them *dialogic systems* and to recognize that students need a number of different types of dialogue in the learning enterprise.

One type of dialogue is dialogue with other students. It fulfils a number of very important functions, including the creation and maintenance of one's image of oneself as a student, establishing resource and personal support networks, and allocating importance to the variety of tasks ahead. The institution can facilitate it by providing contact names, venues, occasions to initiate contact, and so forth.

Another type of dialogue is that which takes place before enrollment with a representative of the institution. This preliminary counseling needs to cover a wide range of areas, such as the prospective student's perceptions of the work required, his or her personal circumstances and timetable, the resources available, his or her study skills, and related matters. Such dialogue can be quite unrelated to the student's intended career, but it is essential if we are to lessen the chances of later dropout or feelings of failure.

The third type of dialogue is the one that most people put first — dialogue with the educator. Here, as with dialogue between students, there are a number of functions that can be fulfilled in appropriate ways. First is the provision of information and facts. Information needs to be provided promptly when it is needed, and access by telephone between student and educator needs to be instant and free. Some countries use voucher systems; these entitle the student to a specified number of long-distance calls. Second is the dialogic conversation that is part and parcel of learning and teaching. Considerable controversy centers on how it should be accomplished. Should tutorials be part of a distance learning program? Much of the controversy has derived from the position and autonomy of teacher and learner in relation to the traditional banking types of distance programs where the individual tutor has a very subsidiary role. But, if we imagine the project-type of program to be the norm, there are clearly key points (at the beginning, for progress reporting, and at the end) when maximum dialogue is likely to be advantageous. Given the purpose, the medium is less important. What is more important is the ability to structure flexibility within time. A one-day meeting or a weeklong summer school are many times more valuable than the same numbers of hours spent singly across a longer period of time.

Media. The preceding comments raise serious questions about media, especially about high-tech media. There is a very real tension between the type of dialogue that we advocate and the increasing use of sophisticated media. Sophistication tends to imply increasing production costs and a corresponding generalization of the material. Further, as Michael Apple (1982) and others have pointed out with respect to schooling, the commercialization of media introduces the ideological perspective of those who prepare the resources and, in order to capture the widest and most profitable market, ensure that it is "noncontroversial."

The time is overdue to begin some critical reappraisal of the media employed in distance education. The same questions have to be asked of every medium: Is it appropriate? Is it cheap and accessible? Does it permit dialogue and autonomy? Does it encourage the learner to interact with it? Does it encourage the learner to link what is being communicated with his or her own knowledge and experience? From the viewpoint of these questions, some books can be as unfriendly as some computers.

Some Broad Issues

As we hinted at the start of this chapter, distance education poses two problems for the radical continuing educator that have barely begun to be addressed in face-to-face education and that are all the more intractable in distance programs: the problem of dialogue and intersubjectivity, and the traditional solitude of the distance learner. In lectures given in Australia, Paulo Freire (1974) described how educators have to liberate themselves from the perspective that defines them as exhaustively preparing material to be taught in advance, then "giving" it to the students as gifts: The subject to be learned, he says, must be "problematical" to both parties. If this challenge has only begun to be met in face-to-face programs, it has barely been acknowledged in distance programs, where not only the preparation but also the teaching goes on the night before. The business of putting holes in the smooth surface of distance programs, of creating room to maneuver is of urgent importance to radical distance educators. The prepackaging of learning programs, often in association with computers, is a familiar and fast-growing trend. Apple (1982) describes the links between this trend and political control of education. It is not enough simply to subvert the system. Teaching around the edges of a tyrannous package is important, but it is not enough. Educators have to look at the technologies that will maximize dialogue and learner autonomy and develop them rather than the currently much more sophisticated technologies of objective setting and knowledge structuring.

As already noted, the second problem for the radical distance educator lies in the traditional solitude of the distance learner. Distance programs are predominantly used by individual students, not by groups. And, for the purposes of radical adult education, the collective dimension is extremely important. There is a real need to develop programs where the learning collective is the participant. Again, technological progress for this end lags well behind.

Involving adult learners in distance education remains a challenge. The extensive, and expensive, effort that has gone into developing distance learning technologies has been in the main in directions that are at best irrelevant, at worst hostile to the interests of radical, empowering, community-based learning. It is our belief that this situation can be altered. Priorities can and must be changed. Technologies can and must be redirected.

References

Anderson, R. A., and Darkenwald, G. G. *Participation and Persistence in American Adult Education.* New York: College Board, 1979.

Apple, M. W. *Education and Power.* Boston: Routledge & Kegan Paul, 1982.

Baath, J. A. "A List of Ideas for the Construction of Distance Education Courses." In D. Sewart, D. J. Keegan, and B. Holmberg (Eds.), *Distance Education: International Perspectives.* London: Croom Helm, 1983.

Belchem, J. "Teaching at a Distance in Britain and New Zealand: Some Early Impressions." *Teaching at a Distance,* 1979, *16,* 2–6.

Bloom, B. S., and others. *Taxonomy of Educational Objectives: The Classification of Educational Goals.* New York: McKay, 1964.

Cross, K. P. *Adults as Learners: Increasing Participation and Facilitating Learning.* San Francisco: Jossey-Bass, 1981.

Davison, J. "Education Counseling in Academic Studies." *Teaching at a Distance,* 1975, *3,* 16–24.

Dodds, A. E., and others. *Distance University Students' Perceptions of the Influences on Their Study.* Murdock University, Western Australia, 1981. (ED 210 000)

Freire, P. *Thinking with Paulo Freire.* A series of tapes made in 1974. Available from Australian Council of Churches, 199 Clarence Street, Sydney, New South Wales, Australia.

Freire, P. *Pedagogy of the Oppressed.* New York: Continuum, 1981.

Harris, D., and Holmes, J. "Openness and Control in Higher Education: Towards a Critique of the Open University." In R. Dale and others, *Schooling and Capitalism.* London: Routledge & Kegan Paul, 1976.

Holmberg, B. *Status and Trends of Distance Education.* London: Kogan Page, 1981.

Holmberg, B. "Guided Didactic Conversation in Distance Education." In *Distance Education: International Perspectives.* London: Croom Helm, 1983.

Keegan, D. J. "On Defining Distance Education." In D. Sewart, D. J. Keegan, and B.

Holmberg (Eds.), *Distance Education: International Perspectives*. London: Croom Helm, 1983.

Moore, M. G. "Toward a Theory of Independent Learning and Teaching." *Journal of Higher Education*, 1973, *44*, 661–679.

Peters, O. "Distance Teaching and Industrial Production: A Comparative Interpretation in Outline." In D. Sewart, D. J. Keegan, and B. Holmberg (Eds.), *Distance Education: International Perspectives*. London: Croom Helm, 1983.

Richardson, P. L. "Adapting Distance Learning for Older Adult Differences." Paper presented at the annual meeting of the American Educational Research Association, Los Angeles, 1981. (ED 210 496)

Sewart, D., Keegan, D. J., and Holmberg, B. (Eds.). *Distance Education: International Perspectives*. London: Croom Helm, 1983.

Michael Law is an adult educator at the University of Waikato, Hamilton, New Zealand. He has long been involved in labor education; he is active in social movements; and he contributes to a distance education program.

Linda Sissons directs research and information services for the New Zealand Federation of Labor. She has been a senior counselor for students in a distance program at the United Kingdom's Open University. In New Zealand, she has published a major distance program for adult educators and worked in distance programs for parents, adult educators, and trade unionists.

To what extent does the participatory nature of discussion make it the continuing education method par excellence?

Discussion as an Effective Educational Method

Stephen Brookfield

Perhaps more than any other method, discussion has come to be regarded as the continuing education method par excellence. In Western Europe and North America in particular, the neighborhood discussion group is the medium for learning that comes closest to being a central, defining feature of the adult education tradition. In the United States, such initiatives as the junto, the lyceum movement, and the Great Books program all used the small discussion group as the central teaching medium. In Canada, the study circles of the Antigonish movement and such activities as the Living Room Learning scheme in British Columbia and the national Farm Forum exhibited a similar reliance on the discussion format. The tutorial class in the British extramural movement has traditionally used discussion for a collaborative consideration of matters of intellectual concern. The purpose of this chapter is to examine the reasons for the exalted status of discussion among continuing educators, to consider some of the uses to which discussion is often put, and to assess the empirical veracity of some benefits claimed for the method by its proponents.

S. H. Rosenblum (Ed.). *Involving Adults in the Educational Process.* New Directions for Continuing Education, no. 26. San Francisco: Jossey-Bass, June 1985.

Rationales for Discussion

Proponents of the discussion method have traditionally claimed a significance for discussion that is societal rather than purely educational. For example, in an early handbook of adult education, Essert (1948) advised Americans to regard membership in a discussion group as a substitute for the spirit and form of the neighborly *gemeinschaft* community that had been lost in the process of twentieth-century urban development. Eduard Lindeman, still the most significant American philosopher of continuing education, urged throughout his professional life that the discussion group be recognized as the pedagogic form uniquely suited to adult education. In *The Meaning of Adult Education,* Lindeman (1926) wrote that discussion was a method that gave students an opportunity to reflect on their experiences and to assign meaning to them in a collaborative quest for understanding. In his article on adult education for the 1930 *Encyclopedia of the Social Sciences* (Lindeman, 1930), he declared that discussion was the distinctive method of adult education in that teacher and taught enjoyed a level of experience that could be used as educational material. In its emphasis on a collaborative mode of learning, discussion served to confirm the democratic nature of adult education.

At the end of World War II, Lindeman (1945) reiterated his belief in the effectiveness of the discussion group as a force for societal rejuvenation. The neighborhood discussion group was not only essential for democratic life, it was also the finest available medium for dealing with controversial issues. Such groups would combat propaganda, develop flexible modes of thought, and encourage the development of natural leadership as a challenge to artificial and arbitrary leadership.

Definitions of Discussion

It is all too easy to talk of the discussion method without clarifying its necessary constituents. There are almost as many definitions of discussion as there are writers who have examined the method. A review of the literature on discussion (Osinki and others, 1972) concluded that definitions of discussion were static, arbitrary, trivial, replete with hidden agendas, and often even fantastic. Because of the diverse meanings that have been attached to discussion, it is important to clarify the ways in which the term is used to avoid the danger of making false comparisons of fundamentally different phenomena.

Definitions of discussion seem to cluster at different points along a continuum distinguished by the degree of control that the teacher exercises over discussion procedures and content. At one end is open or free discussion, the collaborative search for meaning advocated by Lindeman (1930), Paterson (1970), and Bridges (1979). At the other end is controlled discussion — "teaching in which students may raise questions or comment, but the general direction is under the strict control of the teacher" (Bligh, 1972, p. 150). As I shall argue at the end of this chapter, the idea of controlled or guided discussion is a contradiction in terms. A necessary condition of discussion is that there be no preconceived agenda, no cognitive path to be charted, no previously specified objectives either for substantive knowledge to be transmitted or for process features to be exhibited. Hence, guided discussion is conceptual nonsense in that discussion is free and open by definition.

A comparison of definitions reveals that two features are central to most writers' concept of discussion. The first is the idea of purposeful conversation. Group discussion is seen as directed conversation about a topic of mutual interest (Brunner and others, 1959), as purposeful conversation and deliberation (Bergevin and others, 1963), and as conversation with a purpose (Brown, 1975). This first feature of the definition of discussion, then, is concerned with cognitive purpose. The second characteristic of discussion elaborated by most writers is emphatically noncognitive in that it stresses the idea of equal participation. According to these writers an activity is a discussion only if a majority of the group's members participate in verbal exchange. For example, Gulley (1965, p. 4) flatly declares that, "to call an activity discussion, all or most members of the group must participate," and Legge (1971, p. 79) says that the first criterion for an ideal discussion is that "all members would talk together freely and easily, without tensions or inhibitions."

We can see that two features are central to the notion of discussion; these two features are sometimes complementary and sometimes contradictory. The success of discussion sessions can be judged by the extent to which certain cognitive purposes are pursued or by the extent to which all members offer approximately equal verbal contributions. Two separate criteria, then, are applied to judging the value of discussion. One derives from the achievement of certain cognitive ends. The other derives from the extent of participation exhibited by group members.

Discussion and Cognitive Purpose

Defining discussion according to some notion of cognitive purpose raises many problems, principally because the cognitive objectives elaborated by discussion leaders are many and varied. Beard's (1967) survey of 500 university teachers uncovered a broad array of objectives for discussion. These objectives included the clarification of difficult concepts introduced in lectures, the changing of student attitudes, and the encouragement of critically analytic patterns of thought. However, three categories of discussion can be distinguished. Each is oriented toward a different cognitive end.

The first type of discussion is concerned with reaching a decision on some substantive matter. In this type of discussion, the aim is generally clear. Discussions of this nature consider such things as how best to reduce racial conflict in a particular neighborhood or what curricular offerings are appropriate for a continuing education program.

The second type of discussion has as its function the revision of concepts previously encountered in the lecture room or establishing in students' minds an understanding of a new idea, theory, or concept. Bridges (1979) regards discussions of this type as teaching discussions and outlines a variety of pedagogic roles for them. These roles range from arranging times and meeting places for discussion, to acting as chairperson, developing the quality of discourse by questioning participants on the evidence for their opinions, clarifying ambiguous concepts, or illustrating how a particular assertion relates to previous comments. The crucial aspect of such discussions is whether teachers apply the same standards of clarity, conciseness, and supportive evidence to themselves that they apply to students.

The third type of discussion has as its purpose the attainment of affective ends, such as increasing student tolerance or producing attitudinal change. Verner and Booth (1964, p. 83) observe that "discussion is definitely preferred in situations where the learning objective involves group behavioral or attitudinal change." Discussions of this nature seem to contradict the essential condition of discussion in that they are undertaken in order to achieve previously specified objectives. To this extent, they are not free or open discussion but exercises in attitudinal manipulation.

Discussion and Participation

Proponents of the participatory notion of discussion judge whether a discussion has taken place by the amount and diversity of member contributions. Legge's (1971, p. 76) declaration that, "as an educational method in fact, its importance lies in the way in which it impels class members to participate" implies that noncognitive criteria are being used to evaluate the success of discussion and that any educational benefits arising from participation are merely fortunate by-products. If we take this view to its logical conclusion, the group in which all members make verbal contributions of equal length is the quintessential discussion group; the quality and relevance of these contributions are not taken into account.

Stated in this fashion, few if any continuing educators would publicly subscribe to a view of discussion that values participation above quality. However, relative equity of the involvement of group members cannot be removed as a condition of discussion without causing the activity to stop being a discussion in any meaningful sense. Hence, a twelve-member group in which most of the verbal interchange is between three or four members would not be regarded as a "proper" discussion group, whereas a twelve-member group in which ten individuals contributed (even though these contributions were sometimes logically invalid, factually incorrect, or ambiguous) would qualify for such a description. To say this is not to invalidate the use of discussion as a teaching technique; it merely requires that its advocates realize that majority participation is one of the necessary conditions most often proposed.

There are, of course, good educational reasons for emphasizing the participation of all members in discussion. Davis (1961) reported that, as the level of participation in Great Books discussions increased, the dropout rate of inactive as well as of active members decreased. The greater emotional investment required for participation in a discussion group (compared with passive attendance at a lecture) is held to increase identification with the subject matter under consideration. McLeish and others (1973) believe that student involvement generates reflective thinking, while some thirty years ago Sheats and others (1953) observed that adults hold more enduringly and intelligently concepts that they have participated in formulating.

Cognitive Outcomes of Discussion: A Critique

Three cognitive outcomes are typically claimed to result from use of the discussion method. The first outcome concerns the development of powers of analytic clarity. Utterback (1964, p. 132) is typical in his insistence that, "when the object is to stimulate and clarify thinking, discussion is more effective than formal address." Brown (1959) points out that it is through students' attempts to explain a concept, explore an apparent discrepancy between theory and practice, or identify critical issues for discussion that teachers are able to assess their own effectiveness.

The second cognitive benefit of discussion is the increased appreciation of the complexity of a topic that students gain by listening to the different viewpoints expressed by discussion participants. Rogers

(1977) argues that a good discussion inevitably exposes the ambiguities and complexities of a topic. Legge (1971) believes that maturity of judgment concerning the complexity of issues comes to adults through exposure to the many shades of opinion and meaning expressed by discussion members.

The third cognitive benefit of discussion is said to be that it increases students' identification with the subject matter under consideration since it stimulates their interest. Verner and Booth (1964) assert that the increased commitment to learning and identification with subject matter shown by students in discussion proved the superiority of this method over lectures.

The three cognitive outcomes claimed for the discussion method are formidable indeed. If the claims could be substantiated, its status as the continuing education method par excellence would be unassailable. Unfortunately, the topic of discussion is one on which rhetorical exhortation or evangelical fervor can masquerade as considered assessment. A critical examination of discussion procedures and the psychodynamic dimensions of discussions serves to reveal that their nature is often ambiguous.

First, the clarification of thought held to result from such activities as an explanation of a body of knowledge to fellow students is contingent on that explanation's taking place in an emotionally stable setting. Unfortunately, discussion is extremely threatening for many adults. For these individuals, the discussion group is an arena of psychodynamic struggle, a field of emotional battle, particularly when discussion techniques are used in educational contexts characterized by a competitive ethos, for example, in courses where continuous assessment of student "performance" occurs. In this situation—and some kind of informal teacher and peer assessment of performance can be found in many adult classes—students will be alternatively defensive and aggressive. They will be defensive as they interpret critical examinations of their contributions as attacks on themselves, and they will be aggressive as they strive to establish themselves as competent and articulate in their tutor's eyes. In the second context, the quality of discussion will inevitably suffer as the pressure on participants to "contribute for contribution's sake" becomes irresistible. Thus, it is obvious that discussion leaders have a responsibility to set the right climate for discussion at the outset of each session. The training of discussion participants and the establishment of clearly agreed-upon group rules for discussion are obvious prerequisites for discussions characterized by courtesy, openness, and respect for others.

With regard to the enhancement of students' appreciation of the complexities of a given topic, it may well be true that exposure to the diversity of views expressed in a discussion produces this effect. However, the converse can also be the case. The very speed of contribution in some discussion groups is a potential cause of confusion. Since adult education classes, particularly noncredit classes, tend to have an open-door admissions policy, it is not uncommon that discussion participants exhibit a wide range of personalities and abilities. As Cleugh (1970, p. 69) remarks, it will be "the quicker, livelier, more extroverted members who are most stimulated by discussion, while others find it unsatisfactory and muddling." In this situation, a clique of "star" participants emerges whose interaction is viewed by a silent majority of group members.

A general difficulty facing discussion participants, no matter how articulate they are, results from the time that elapses between making a connection between another discussant's remark and the relevant knowledge or insight that one possesses, mentally rehearsing one's contribution before articulation, and finally offering one's contribution to the group. This process of connection and rehearsal can so absorb the participant's attention that the discussion has progressed significantly beyond the point on which the participant wishes to contribute by the time he or she actually speaks. This means that the comments will be perceived as irrelevant to the discussion by the time they are expressed.

The Psychodynamics of Discussion

In emphasizing the participation of students as a criterion for judging the success of discussion, it is easy to focus on the amount of student interaction without considering its quality. The study by Ruddock and Morris (1955) of discussion patterns in a six-meeting continuing education class on the psychology of everyday life graphically demonstrates the folly of separating these two features. An average 79 percent of the participants' contributions were judged irrelevant in terms of the specific issues to be addressed, although most were in the general area selected for discussion. The authors noted no discernible coherent progression in questions or opinions and reported that students shared very unequally in the discussion. A particularly interesting finding concerned the manner in which student participation averages were quickly reached. Half of the members of the group reached their average number of contributions in the opening meeting, and 85 percent had reached that level by the third session. Of seven individuals who were silent during half or more than half of the meetings, five had been silent at one or both of the first two sessions.

One of the criticisms that students most forcefully voice of discussion concerns the manner in which domineering students use discussion groups as a forum for the reinforcement of their self-esteem. More than 20 percent of the students in Hill's (1960) comparison of the effectiveness of lecture and discussion methods complained about overly loquacious students. Kaplan's (1960) study of 118 liberal arts adults discussion groups also recorded dissatisfaction with discussion methods that did not curb overtalkative, domineering students.

The discussion group is often described as the quintessential example of collaborative learning in which groups of adults engage in a cooperative endeavor to learn from one another. In reality, taking part in a discussion group can be a highly threatening experience in which discussion is seen as a competitive emotional battleground. The idea of the discussion group as a forum in which individuals can compete to attain star status in the eyes of both peers and tutors is partly a reflection of broad cultural values. Our culture puts great emphasis on the extrovert, on other-directed individuals, and the person who is seen and heard in an educational setting will usually be regarded as an educational success in comparison to a quiet colleague.

Since participants invest discussion sessions with an emotional significance, any perceived attack on individual self-esteem is likely to be forcefully repelled. Hence, a critical comment on a member's contribution in an emotionally charged atmosphere will be treated as an act of aggression in the competition for status and result in substantial discord. Utterback (1964, p. 97) describes this danger as follows: "In discussion we are likely... to respond emotionally to any remark that contradicts what we have said, that questions our motives, or that seems in any other way to attack us personally. Our resentment against the speaker then blinds us to the merit we might otherwise see in his argument."

Distinct from the whole question of individual competition for positions in the discussion pecking order are the broad issues raised by the tendency of groups to silence deviant opinions that threaten consensual norms. For example, Gulley (1965) notes how communications tend to be directed toward deviates up to the point where group members decide that these person's views cannot be reconciled with the majority view. At this point, communications to such individuals cease, or the individuals are actually expelled from the group.

Because groups tend to strive over time for a sense of cohesion, it is quite likely, as Fawcett Hill (1969) maintains, that members may become so enamored of group cohesiveness that the goals of the group may become obscured. Deviants perform an important function in preventing this by drawing attention to inconvenient facts or theories, thereby guarding against the possibility of the group's becoming intellectually static. Discussion leaders thus have an important responsibility to protect minority opinions and to remind the group that extended conflict or the articulation of unpopular, minority opinions should not automatically be perceived as negative. Bridges (1979) points out that this tendency is particularly noticeable in decision-making discussions, which generally fall short of meeting the criteria for open discussions. It may not be possible to pursue consensus and preserve openness at the same time in such discussions, and at some point divergent views and dissenting opinions have to be silenced so that a decision can be reached. Bridges's concern is that discussion leaders are too intolerant of extended conflict and that this silencing will happen too quickly.

Conclusion: The Conditions for Discussion

We have seen that discussion occupies a unique status in the hierarchy of continuing education methods. In practically every initiative dear to the hearts of continuing educators—junto, Great Books program, Highlander folk school, Farm Forum, Antigonish movement, extramural tutorial classes, the Danish Folk High School, Freirean culture circles—the discussion group has constituted the methodological heart. Eduard Lindeman (1926, p. 31) proclaimed the discussion group to be "the setting for adult education, the modern quest for life's meaning." In their overview of adult education research, Brunner and others (1959) argued that discussion was used for its own sake because of the generally favorable attitude it invoked in the minds of American adult educators. In Britain, Paterson (1970, p. 28) noted that generalizations about the nature, role, and value of discussion currently formed "chief articles of the catechism in which novices to liberal adult education are expected to verse themselves." Finally, Houle (1972) has succinctly summarized the reasons for the ubiquity of discussion in continuing education practice. For Houle, discussion has been adopted because it is regarded as the best medium through which adults can explore their experience. This exploration of experience is held to be the essential purpose of adult education, and discussion is thus viewed as the best method to use in all circumstances.

If one theme has emerged from this analysis of the disjunction between the rhetorical exhortations of discussion proponents and the reality of adult education discussion sessions, it is that discussions do not exhibit equity of participation and intellectual elegance simply because a tutor has decreed that a group is to engage in discussion. Crucial to the success of discussion sessions is the acquisition by participants of appropriate, consensually agreed-upon behaviors. Continuing educators will sometimes blithely introduce discussion at the outset of a course to adults who have probably not been required to participate publicly in a shared consideration of ideas since their schooldays (and possibly not even then). In these circumstances, it is not surprising to find that the resultant discussion is characterized by intolerance, meandering, or simple refusal to participate.

Miller (1964) believes that participant training is so crucial to success in adult discussion groups that the first sessions in any discussion-based course should be devoted to evolving procedural rules and codes of conduct that can guide members in subsequent meetings. Only then will the epistemological underpinnings of discussion proposed by Bridges (1979) — that all members (including leaders) must respect the opinions of others and that all members must be skeptical of their own as well as of others' authority — be discernible in actual discussion sessions.

Bridges (1979) has also evolved a moral culture for group dicussion that comprises six ethical principles to be accepted by participants as the tacit assumptions underlying their engagement in discussion: reasonableness (openness to others' arguments and perspectives), peaceableness and orderliness, truthfulness, freedom, equality, and respect for persons. This moral culture and the epistemological underpinnings already discussed provide the foundation for open discussion in which subject matter, group membership, time for group talk, and learning outcomes are open. Those engaged in such open discussion have a responsibility to set aside their own prejudices and to entertain imaginative speculation.

It is this form of discussion that I wish to propose as the quintessential adult education method. In a seminal paper, Paterson (1970) conducted a masterly analysis of the concept of discussion. In his view, discussion is the educational activity par excellence, an educational end in itself requiring no further justification. To Paterson, participation in discussion is a characteristically human activity of the most intimate and fundamental kind in which individual adults commit and discover their whole being. Hence, "to address others in discussion. . . is to bear witness to one's own attempt to reconstruct one's experience meaningfully, and it is at the same time to invite others to share this reconstructed experience" (Paterson, 1970, p. 37).

To this extent, the cognitive benefits mentioned previously as accruing from participation in discussion are by-products, albeit educationally useful ones, of the true significance of discussion. As argued earlier, the concept of guided discussion must be considered self-negating. In Paterson's (1970, p. 47) words, "true discussion cannot be directed or even guided, for to attempt to do so is in effect to opt out of the discussion, to close one's consciousness to alternative interpretations of the phenomenon under discussion before these alternatives have ever been stated."

To participate in this authentic form of mutual address, in this collaborative search for meaning, requires personal courage and analytic ability of a high order. It requires adults to be willing to examine the social origins of many of their beliefs critically, to be aware of how many of the assumptions formulating their conduct have been acquired from external sources and authorities, such as parents, schoolteachers, and peers, and hence to view their dearly held meaning systems as provisional and relative. In this sense, to participate in discussion — in the collaborative externalization, exploration, and critical analysis of personally significant meaning systems — is to realize one's adulthood to its fullest extent.

Four conditions can be identified that, if they are met, are likely to enhance the chances that good (that is, meaningful and productive) discussions will occur. First, group members need to devise and to subscribe to an appropriate moral culture for group discussion. In simple terms, this means that the group must spend some time agreeing upon a set of procedural rules concerning the manner in which equity of participation is to be realized. Second, discussion leaders can exercise a degree of forethought regarding the selection of materials that are to form the substantive focus of group discussions. The question to be discussed should not be too factual or uncontroversial, nor should it be able to be answered in the course of preparatory reading for the group. Third, the leader should be well versed both in the subject matter to be covered during the discussion and in the principles of group dynamics. Only someone skilled at dealing with the problems of apparent isolates, pressure to silence deviants, and attempts to use the group as a mechanism for bolstering self-esteem can be said to be an effective discussion leader.

Fourth, discussion participants can be prepared for discussion not only through the generation and acceptance of a moral culture for discussion sessions but also through the development of reasoning skills (so that inconsistencies and ambiguities in argument can be detected) and through the improvement of communication abilities (so that ideas can be articulated accurately). In providing a forum for the pursuit and realization of these higher-order intellectual skills as well as in requiring participants to evolve a democratic, moral culture for group discourse, the discussion method can indeed be claimed to be the adult education method par excellence.

66

References

Beard, R. *Small-Group Discussion in University Teaching.* London: Department of Higher Education, University of London, 1967.

Bergevin, P., Morris, D., and Smith, R. M. *Adult Education Procedures: A Handbook of Tested Patterns for Effective Participation.* Greenwich, Conn.: Seabury Press, 1963.

Bligh, D. A. *What's the Use of Lectures?* Harmondsworth: Penguin, 1972.

Bridges, D. *Education, Democracy, and Discussion.* Windsor, Berkshire: NFER Publishing, 1979.

Brown, G. "Techniques of Discussion." In J. Rogers (Ed.), *Teaching on Equal Terms.* London: B.B.C. Publications, 1959.

Brown, G. *Microteaching: A Programme of Teaching Skills.* London: Methuen, 1975.

Brunner, E. de S., Wilder, D. S., Kirchner, C., and Newberry, J. S. *An Overview of Adult Education Research.* Chicago: Adult Education Association of the U.S.A., 1959.

Cleugh, M. *Educating Older People.* London: Tavistock, 1970.

Davis, J. A. *Great Books and Small Groups.* Englewood Cliffs, N.J.: Free Press, 1961.

Essert, P. L. "The Discussion Group in Adult Education in America." In M. L. Ely (Ed.), *Handbook of Adult Education in the United States.* New York: Teachers College, Columbia University, 1948.

Fawcett Hill, W. M. *Learning Through Discussion.* Beverly Hills, Calif.: Sage, 1969.

Gulley, H. E. *Discussion, Conference, and Group Process.* New York: Holt, Rinehart and Winston, 1965.

Hill, R. J. *A Comparative Study of Lecture and Discussion Methods.* White Plains, N.Y.: Fund for Adult Education, 1960.

Houle, C. O. *The Design of Education.* San Francisco: Jossey-Bass, 1972.

Kaplan, A. *Study Discussion in the Liberal Arts.* White Plains, N.Y.: Fund for Adult Education, 1960.

Legge, D. "Discussion Methods." In G. W. Roderick and M. D. Stephens (Eds.), *Teaching Techniques in Adult Education.* Newton Abbott, Devon: David & Charles, 1971.

Lindeman, E. C. L. *The Meaning of Adult Education.* New York: New Republic, 1926.

Lindeman, E. C. L. "Adult Education." In *Encyclopedia of the Social Sciences.* Vol. 1. New York: Macmillan, 1930.

Lindeman, E. C. L. "World Peace Through Adult Education." *The Nation's Schools,* 1945, *35* (3), 23.

McLeish, J., Matheson, W., and Park, J. *The Psychology of the Learning Group.* London: Hutchinson, 1973.

Miller, H. L. *Teaching and Learning in Adult Education.* New York: Macmillan, 1964.

Osinski, F. W. W., Ohliger, J., and McCarthy, C. *Toward Gog and Magog; or, A Critical Review of the Literature of Group Discussion.* Syracuse, N. Y.: Syracuse University Publications in Continuing Education/ERIC Clearinghouse on Adult Education, 1972.

Paterson, R. W. K. "The Concept of Discussion: A Philosophical Approach." *Studies in Adult Education,* 1970, *2* (1), 28–50.

Rogers, J. *Adults Learning.* Milton Keynes: Open University Press, 1977.

Ruddock, R., and Morris, J. F. "Discussion in a W.E.A. Class: A Qualitative Analysis." *Adult Education* (U.K.), 1955, *28* (3), 200–210.

Sheats, P., Jayne, C., and Spence, R. (Eds.). *Adult Education: The Community Approach.* New York: Dryden Press, 1953.

Utterback, W. E. *Group Thinking and Conference Leadership.* New York: Holt, Rinehart and Winston, 1964.

Verner, C., and Booth, A. *Adult Education.* New York: Center for Applied Research in Applied Education, 1964.

Stephen Brookfield is assistant professor of adult and continuing education at Teachers College, Columbia University. He was professor of adult education at the University of British Columbia and research officer for the United Kingdom Advisory Council for Adult and Continuing Education.

Liberating education involves learning associated with the struggle to survive in a world not organized in the interests of the majority.

Involving Adults in Social Change Education

Michael Law
Linda Sissons

Social change is one of those overworked phrases that adult educators like to use. It implies progress. Thus, *social change education* sounds progressive, even when it is used to describe learning how to adapt to a social environment shaped by others. When we use the phrase *social change education,* we are referring to liberating education: education that implies social transformation and that is designed to find answers to fundamental social issues.

The urgent need to find answers to critical social problems transcends national boundaries. Industrial development, the arms race, the economic crisis, and natural disasters have all produced problems that threaten the planet. Developing an awareness of the enormity of the problems facing humankind and mobilizing people to confront and overcome them is an educational challenge. It is a challenge that should excite concerned continuing educators.

Yet, at the very moment when radical, social change education is desperately required, many practitioners are pessimistic. Concerned practitioners, perhaps soured by past experience, seem to doubt that continuing education can really contribute to meaningful social change.

S. H. Rosenblum (Ed.). *Involving Adults in the Educational Process.* New Directions for Continuing Education, no. 26. San Francisco: Jossey-Bass, June 1985.

Certainly there are grounds for pessimism. Many of the old assumptions about social change are clearly not true. In the industrialized countries, reformed welfare capitalism has not provided a sound basis for sustained economic and social justice; access to education has not empowererd the majority of people. Much of what is called continuing education has become increasingly entrepreneurial. So lucrative are selected vocational and recreational programs that private enterprise has moved in to skim the cream off the profits.

Nevertheless, we find it encouraging to discover that colleagues in several countries are responding to this dismal situation by asking harder, sharper questions about current theory and practice. As radical critiques developed elsewhere in the social sciences are applied to continuing education, there is a growing recognition of the possibility of a pedagogy of mobilization. Continuing education itself is being redefined in a way that recognizes the educational potential of everyday struggles.

What is beginning to emerge is a view of educational possibilities that is critical, hopeful, positive, and realistic. This chapter seeks to contribute to the growing dialogue. Our aim is to make sense of practice. We believe that involving ourselves and others in social change education requires us as educators to become involved in a dialogical way not just with people engaged in everyday struggles but also with the struggles themselves (Law and Sissons, 1984).

We begin by outlining views about individuals and the individual's relationship to society. In our work, we have found it necessary to reexamine critically the assumptions about individuals and society that underpinned the adult education theory we were taught in British and North American graduate programs. We are attempting to understand continuing education within the context of the wider social relations of which it is a part. In the second section of this chapter, we explore ideas about continuing education for social change. We attempt to identify arenas in which concerned practitioners can make useful contributions. Finally, we illustrate our general points with specific case studies. If there are underlying themes running through this chapter, they are commitment and dialogue. Involving adults in social change education is not simply a matter of technique; educators must involve themselves in the struggle for a better world.

Individual and Society

A social change perspective regards individuals as active agents: people who, acting in concert with others, can transform social relations. This perspective implies an awareness of social context and a conception of humans as social beings. In our view, these two ideas are intertwined.

We think of humans as social beings in two ways. First, they are social in terms of needs. As with all biological animals, humans have immediate physical needs. In order to satisfy those needs, humans must produce. But, human production extends beyond the satisfaction of immediate needs; as humans work they create new needs. The satisfaction of hunger with cooked food provides a simple example. It creates the need for a means to cook the food. Similarly, satisfying the need for warmth by wearing clothes creates the need for clothing.

As humans have developed increasingly complex social relations, an ever expanding range of needs has evolved. These days, very few people satisfy their needs directly through their own efforts; most work for money and then use that money to purchase the means of satisfying their needs. Thus, in a very fundamental way, economic relationships define one of the senses in which humans are social beings. And, as the economies of the world become more interdependent, human social relationships become more universal.

The second sense in which humans are social beings is more complex; it relates to ideas, attitudes, desires, and forms of behavior. Insofar as it is concerned with acts of cognition, with learning, this second sense may be seen as being more directly related to education.

We believe that an important characteristic of human life is the way in which each generation builds in the ideas, attitudes, desires, and forms of behavior that previous generations or contemporaries have created. Such words and phrases as *knowledge, culture, social norms, acceptable behavior,* and even *common sense* all refer to aspects of this process of building in. Building-in occurs throughout everyday life. The family, church, formal schooling, and the workplace all contain what has become known as a hidden curriculum — learning to conform to social norms. Mass culture plays an important role in popularizing and reinforcing these norms, through the media, movies, and sport. In other words, how people interpret themselves, the world, and their place in the world is socially constituted. In modern societies, the process of acquiring these interpretations is such that it is unreal to talk about personality traits as independent, individual characteristics. Hence, we are skeptical of the emphasis that mainstream continuing education places on inner drives, instincts, and self-direction.

The importance of the ideas we have been discussing is highlighted when these ideas are linked to those of people like Paulo Freire (1981). Freire has pointed to the political dimension of knowledge; he argues that ideas, attitudes, desires, and forms of behavior are not neutral. In any society, these concepts reflect those of the dominant forces. In other words, people build in or internalize the worldview of the very forces that oppress them.

Adaptive Continuing Education

It is in the context just outlined that we critique the adaptive character of mainstream continuing education theory and practice. Often, even what is sometimes described as social change education is adaptive in that it entrenches conformity with the existing social order. In part, this is a historical problem. The reformist tradition in continuing education has its origins in the liberal progressive movement of the early decades of this century. Educators like Mansbridge and Tawney in England and Lindeman in the United States regarded adult education as playing an important role in finding a middle path between unbridled capitalism and revolutionary socialism. In brief, these reformers believed that, if people could be educated to exercise their constitutional rights, form pressure groups, and secure the election of sympathetic legislators, then the poor and the weak would secure the political power that could counterbalance the economic power of the large capitalists. The key to achieving these ends was to be the education of the individual. The reformist tradition linked the betterment of society with individual growth (Darkenwald and Merriam, 1982).

In recent years, the idea of individual growth has received increasing attention. The main theoretical work in continuing education contains two elements: One emphasizes the pressures of society and asks what roles adults have to fill and therefore what competencies they need. The other looks from the viewpoint of the developing individual. This second element incorporates many of the ideas of the life cycle theorists; it assumes a growth trajectory that begins at birth and that lasts until death. It asks what the characteristics and impulses of adult growth stages are and what learning needs these imply.

The concept of needs is central to mainstream theory, research, and practice. Some needs are inferred from social roles and responsibilities—parent, worker, spouse, club member, citizen, and so forth. Judgments are made about the adequacy of role performance; discrepancies between actual and desired performance are then identified as needs. Other needs are derived from the "third force" tendency in humanistic psychology, from the theories of Maslow, Rogers, and R. W. White. The emphasis there is on equilibrium or congruence, on feeling good about oneself and one's place in the world. Just as various religious movements hold out the promise of personal salvation, popular humanistic psychology promises personal liberation, self-actualization without the necessity of social change.

These theoretical assumptions find expression in continuing education programs that are sometimes labeled "social change." One popular approach is the upward-mobility model. This model assumes that access to higher status, income, and power is a result of educational attainment and seeks to improve access by offering a second chance to gain formal qualifications. If the mechanical barriers are removed, it is argued, then educational attainment will be more evenly spread through the social classes, ethnic groups, and genders.

In this model, success is defined in terms of prevailing values. Social change is seen simply as a means of getting more working people, minorities, or women into high-status roles. The assumptions underpinning the model are naive. While educational attainment may well correlate with success, it is not the only relevant factor. Pierre Bourdieu (Bourdieu and Passeron, 1977) points to all the other social and cultural advantages that favor those with high social class status; he calls these advantages "cultural capital." Other writers, such as Apple (1979), Bowles and Gintis (1976), and Giroux (1981, 1983), point to the relationship between educational attainment and social class. Some of these ideas are now being applied to continuing education, for example by Gelpi (1979) and Thompson (1980, 1983); we have applied them in our own work (Law and Sissons, 1984). While these writers have differing emphases, their work takes into account the power relationships that the traditional upward-mobility model consistently ignores.

Of course some individuals do make it, and most adult educators can point to success stories. But, in our experience such individuals generally only succeed by detaching themselves from their social peers. They go it alone. There is no collective change in the status or in the class situation of their peers.

A second approach to social change education is the helping/coping model. This approach has found favor with many disillusioned practitioners who have become frustrated with the failure of education to empower people whom they see as disadvantaged. Blending social work with adult education, this model views continuing education as essentially concerned with helping individuals to adapt to the demands of life, to cope with the problems of poverty, ill-health, and life crisis and transitions. In recent years, this approach has been employed to address social problems arising from economic crisis and technological change.

Programs for unemployed people are an example. These programs usually begin with the assumption that the reason why people are unemployed is that they lack certain skills or have "bad" attitudes. Accordingly, the emphasis is on job training, attitudinal change, or both. The problem is recognized as a group problem, but it is then attributed to personal deficiencies. The victim is blamed for his or her disadvantage. Like the social mobility model, the helping/coping approach accepts the world as a given. It says that we cannot do much about the world and its injustices, but we can pick up the pieces. The problem, of course, is that the number of social casualties increases as the pace of society quickens.

Adaptative continuing education reaffirms a predefined social framework by accepting popular myths about equality of opportunity and the potential for democratic participation. The situations in which individuals find themselves are regarded simply as personal grievances. Unemployment, eviction, local pollution, ill-health, violence in the home, and so on are localized. The political dimension is obscured.

Continuing Education and Social Change

As we discussed earlier, humans are social beings. It follows that personal grievances do not exist independent of the social context, nor is the way in which they are perceived, either by the grievant or others, independent of the building in of ideas that we considered earlier, So, as Heller (1982) has suggested, learning how to translate a personal grievance into a social issue itself leads halfway to the accomplishment of liberation; recognizing a problem's social dimensions points to the need for social solutions.

The second phase of liberating education lies in working for the resolution of social issues. The radical potential of a social issue is not so much the issue itself but the steps that have to be taken to resolve it. While it may be possible through reform to alleviate unemployment, racism, sexism, or even localized pollution, the fundamental causes of these problems cannot be tackled on a one-to-one basis. To eliminate these and other evils, it is necessary to change social relations radically. It would be naive to suggest that social relations are going to be changed overnight; they are not. So, if liberating education requires political power and the oppressed have none, how is it possible to engage in transformative education prior to the advent of social change? Freire (1981) addresses this question. He cites the potential of "educational projects," the cognitive aspects of liberating education, and the need for an action dimension.

What are the salient core characteristics of a social change educational project? We suggest there are four: First, liberating education should have as its goal collective empowerment, which is action oriented. Second, access should be for the economically, socially, and culturally oppressed. Third, control needs to involve participant decision making within the context of a cooperative group pursuing collective goals and methods. Finally, the curriculum should be holistic; it needs to locate the specific subject matter within a historical and social context, and it should involve a mix of skills development and understanding oriented toward action for social change (Sissons and Law, 1982).

Having outlined the skeleton of a model, we must identify where and how such liberating education might take place. We believe that a realistic, practical approach requires educators to take advantage of the opportunities that present themselves in the real world in which they live. Even in the context of formal education, spaces and cracks do exist. As our case studies will show, people are taking advantage of opportunities within the system.

Another important educational arena is that of popular struggles. We suggest that there is enormous educational potential within peoples' movements. A view of education that distinguishes between education and political agitation has caused its potential to be underestimated in the past. Within popular movements, important learnings occur in the course of struggle. Activists acquire organizational skills necessary to establish and sustain an action group; they learn political skills to lobby a congressperson or to take on city hall, and they learn people skills—how to popularize an issue and mobilize support. In the process, those involved in the campaign learn a great deal about the issue itself; some begin to make connections between their campaign and others. Some continuing education agencies may already contribute to this process by helping activists to develop some of the skills just mentioned.

However, social change education extends beyond teaching people organizational skills. What gives social action its change potential is the idea of movement; participants can realize that their particular set of demands forms part of a wider struggle for a better world. In our experience with single-issue campaigns, there is a tendency for social action to be localized. While many people work very hard to win an improvement here or a concession there, the link between one campaign and another is often broken. Of course, it is usually in the best interests of those with power in society to ensure that the link is broken, to divide and rule. Educators who are involved in popular struggles can contribute usefully by working within movements to broaden understanding of the causes that give rise to particular concerns and of the interrelationships among movements. The peace movement, for example, is also implicitly about jobs, racism, sexism, and the exploitation of people in Third World countries.

Social Change Education: Some Case Studies

To illustrate the points made so far, we present some case studies. Some of the cases contain both reformist and transformist elements; none may be considered especially remarkable. However, they reflect the practical experiences of continuing educators who have tried to make sense of their practice and apply it. Some of the cases are from the literature; we know others from personal involvement or contact. While our examples are drawn from several countries, we believe that what has been done in one industrial country could be tried in any other.

Critical Teaching in an Institutional Setting. Ira Shor is an English professor at The College of Staten Island of the City University of New York. After some years of experimenting, he outlined a number of very useful strategies in his book *Critical Teaching and Everyday Life* (Shor, 1980). Shor has attempted to apply Freire's ideas in a North American classroom. His students are worker students, most of whom study part-time.

Shor suggests that educators find some familiar item drawn from mass culture that can provoke students to engage in deep social analysis. His suggestions include the hamburger. Following Shor's method, we have used this approach in classroom settings in New Zealand. First, students were asked to study the item itself in great detail. Focusing on a Big Mac, students noted its food content, commented on its nutritional qualities, assessed value for money, and compared it with other, similar items. They explored the idea of junk food. Next, they examined the item in the context of its social setting. An interesting discussion emerged that built on the different responses of teenage students and older students in the group. For the younger class members, McDonalds was a natural part of their lives. But, for the older students their involvement with McDonalds came through its pitch to their children. These and a host of other discoveries about the way in which McDonalds promotes its product led to a stimulating discussion about the way in which this and other franchise operations had become an accepted part of contemporary New Zealand culture.

The third step of Shor's method involves global analysis. Because we were fortunate to have overseas students in the class, we were able to assess the impact of McDonalds in other countries as well as in our own. It was during this discussion that students established the link between implementation of the McDonalds type of franchise and the introduction of mass television. They concluded that fast-food chains would not be viable without television, since it was saturation television advertising that had created the market demand. Shor's fourth step, locating the item in time, brought this earlier discovery into sharper perspective. Again, it was the older class members who recalled life before McDonalds and Colonel Sanders. In New Zealand, take-out food used to be prepared in small, neighborhood-based, family-owned shops; this was true even of the first generation of hamburger bars. But, with the implantation of mass-producing franchise chains, the family shops often went out of business. The final step in the analytical process was to examine the item over a longer time span; this revealed the ways in which people's eating habits had changed and how food service had become more commercialized.

These experiments produced a variety of learnings. At the general level, they stimulated discussion about the way in which franchise chains have penetrated the New Zealand economy. More important perhaps, they prompted participants to explore the ways in which they themselves had become caught up in the fast-food culture, either directly as consumers themselves or indirectly through their children. Some participants were quite shocked to realize the extent to which television advertising had penetrated their own consciousness. For example, during a discussion about the content of the meat patty, one student found herself using the words of a commercial before she realized it.

Shor also suggests using creative writing as part of the process of developing this critique. In our own experiments, we have asked groups of students to write collective essays using the five stages suggested by Shor as headings. The resulting essays have been shared among all class members. This collective approach is not just a way of promoting cooperation; it stimulates good small-group discussion and analysis.

Choosing items from everyday life, from mass culture, enables participants to relate to the consumer product under consideration; it is part of their real world. The process that Shor recommends is very similar to the generative themes and thematic fans that Freire describes. The model enables participants to make links. We have been encouraged by comments from students that exercises like the one just described have prompted them to engage in similar analysis of other aspects of their everyday life.

Of course, it would be romantic to get overexcited about this type of experiment. What is important about Shor's work and our own experiences with Shor's approach is that it shows that it is possible in classroom situations to begin to undo some of the brainwashing that occurs in modern societies. Participants can be encouraged to develop some critical thinking.

University Extension. In *Learning Liberation: Women's Response to Men's Education,* British adult educator Jane Thompson (1983) reported on the Southampton experiment called Second Chance. A serious and committed program for women, Second Chance aimed to offer an introduction to law, literature, sociology, politics and history in a form that was uncommon in university adult education. What distinguished this program from the traditional program were the target group and the learning processes evolved within the program.

Second Chance was advertised as explicitly for working-class women. Intended participants were interviewed; during the interviews, the traditional clientele was screened out. Further, this was "'serious education,' not the 'low-profile' variety which gets smuggled by stealth into community centres" (Thompson, 1983, p. 152). A comprehensive, systematic, and quite lengthy program, it made heavy demands on participants and organizers alike. Most important of all, it had been designed as a liberating educational project. From the outset, those involved with the program made the political character of the course unmistakably clear.

Like Ira Shor, Thompson and her colleagues found that purposeful writing played a significant part in the learning process. She commented: "the aims of the writers' workshops are not to encourage creative writing as such.... The main concern is to explore the condition of being a woman in our society through discussion and personal writing about firsthand experience. The experiences which women choose to write about become the experiences discussed and shared within the groups and have included, among others, childhood memories, working lives, relationships with men, low income, family life, depression, and repression" (Thompson, 1983, p. 167).

Although Thompson emphasizes that the program's focus was similar to that of many other developments in women's studies, we suggest that a number of factors make Second Chance a useful case study: first, the explicitly working-class focus; second, the clear political perspective of the content; third, its development within an existing and educationally conservative institution; fourth, the way in which the organizers and the participants developed appropriate learning processes; fifth, the manner in which those involved have conscientiously documented their work and located it within the context of broad discussion about women's response to men's education.

Community Education. In a small, isolated New Zealand town, one of our colleagues, Trevor Mallard, worked from a community education base to develop a learning project for young, unemployed Maori (indigenous Polynesian) youth, most of whom were members of a street gang known as the Mongrel Mob. The young people's immediate needs included useful employment. Since most had prison records and were early school leavers with few work skills, they were generally classified as unemployable (Taumarunui Work Trust, 1983).

Mallard worked with the young people to examine their situation. Out of these discussions emerged a cooperative work scheme, the Taumarunui Work Trust, which obtained several work contracts from the local county, which in turn was reimbursed from the central government's relief funds. The work was essentially laboring, such as clearing trees along riverbanks. Ironically, the main beneficiaries were local farmers, generally political supporters of the then government. This helped to legitimize the work trust. It also provided space in which political education could develop.

From the outset, the emphasis in the Trust was on cooperative decision making that built on the democratic decision-making structures of the street gang. Further, unlike similar projects elsewhere, the members in this scheme did not confuse their technically self-employed status with social reality. The group voluntarily unionized and observed union contract conditions and procedures; shop stewards were elected, and correct dispute procedures were followed. Thus, each worker was both part of the collective and an individual with full union rights.

Involvement with the union meant involvement in the political and economic issues with which the union movement was concerned. Work trust members played an active role in local union affairs, participated in labor education programs, and helped to strengthen the general level of political awareness in the town. Other educational activity focused on work skills needed in order to apply for work contracts; it also included mini learning projects around such themes as racism, sexism, economic relationships, the place of alcohol and cigarettes in trust members' lives, relations with the police, and so forth. However, the principal learnings came from the total experience. Among the most significant of these was a questioning of traditional supervisory patterns at the workplace — a realization that bosses were not necessary.

Employment Skills Programs. Earlier, we discussed the myth of social mobility, which is a cornerstone of the ideology of free enterprise. Success is individualized, attributed to personal skills, initiative, luck, and pluck. By implication, failure is also an individual problem; the person is "in deficit." Unemployed young people, especially ethnic minorities, have been hurt most cruelly by this notion. Young people are often blamed for their own predicament. In most Western countries, there is a pattern to identification both of the "problem" and of the so-called solution: skills training, adult basic education, programs to facilitate the transition from school to work. Following the lead of Britain, New Zealand launched in 1983 a modular program cynically entitled School Leavers Training and Employment Preparation Scheme — STEPS.

Some progressive educators were scornful of the scheme and avoided having anything to do with it. In Rotorua, a mid–North Island city, a group of local community organizations decided to take this government-financed scheme and transform it. They concluded that unemployment was a structural, not a personal, problem; they noted that the burden of unemployment was falling most heavily on those who were least able to bear it: the young, Maori and Pacific Islanders, and women. They concluded that this was because of racism, sexism, and the class location of Maori and Pacific Islanders. On the basis of this analysis, they defined their aims and resolved "that the most important aspects of the program be centered on developing in ourselves and the young people self-awareness, personal growth, *aroha* (love) towards yourself and others, commitment to being rather than having, and a range of other qualities, such as responsibility, discipline, and commitment" (Puawai, 1983, p. 1).

From this critical reappraisal emerged Puawai, a program that involved a deliberate restructuring of STEPS. An important change was to break out of the module system, which shunted the young people around different training agencies. Instead, Puawai kept groups of young people together at four home bases; this prevented the fragmentation that the module system fosters and made it possible for a collective identity to develop. Each home base was a community house, and most of the team workers were drawn from the local community.

Learning to make collective decisions and working together to achieve the goals set were important aspects of the young adults' learnings within Puawai. In the process of discussing projects, the young people began to develop some understanding of the causes of the nature of their situation. Within the project, there was special emphasis on developing the young adults' identity as Maori and on breaking down stereotypes with respect to gender roles.

Puawai came under enormous pressure from the government bureaucracy. It was not particularly radical; many of its goals were specifically adaptive. But, it did more than simply provide young people with a better alternative. Projects like this also contribute to the wider political debate by directly challenging popular myths about unemployed young people. The learning approach that the project adopted challenged individualistic styles of work; it promoted collectivity and the development of collective understanding. Finally, it and other projects like it provide evidential support for demands for educational alternatives.

Labor Education. We believe that some of the cracks and spaces we discussed earlier can be found in labor education. Since late 1983, Linda Sissons and Ray Harbridge have developed a new dimension to labor education in New Zealand by producing a number of simple video films (Sissons and Harbridge, 1984). The first dealt with changes in industrial law. These changes and political opportunism on the part of the then-governing party had prompted a complicated, highly charged debate. Sissons and Harbridge, along with Trish Sarr, made a simple, low-budget thirteen-minute video that outlined the main issues and discussed their effects. The issues demanded some explanatory content, but the emphasis was on the effects of the new legislation on workers. Rather than have only experts describe these, the producers filmed shop stewards and rank-and-file workers.

The first film was so well received that three more were made in the space of five months. All dealt with topical issues; all addressed the political aspects of these issues. The films were not designed to be shown as documentaries; rather, they were intended as "trigger" films, as something to start discussion.

In reviewing our experiences with these videos, we found that the really positive element was the involvement of workers on film. When other workers viewed the videos, they saw people like themselves analyzing and discussing issues that the regular media tended to represent as being high-level and complicated. The primary learnings developed through dialogue in the discussions that followed showings of the video. In effect, an instrument of mass culture, television, was being transformed into a tool for countereducation. The form was the same, but the content and the commentators were different. Workers thus began to realize that fundamental economic and political issues were the legitimate subject of popular debate, that they did not need to accept passively the received wisdom presented by the media.

Independent Labor Education. The North American experience is rich with examples of independent labor education. A rank-and-file organization of autoworkers, the Independent Skilled Trade Council, is a good contemporary example. Since the 1970s, the I.S.T.C. has been organizing around issues that concern American auto workers: contract conditions, the introduction of new technology, the establishment of quality circles in auto plants, and, more recently, concessions and givebacks.

What strikes us about the I.S.T.C.'s work is the strong educational dimension. The council adopts a holistic approach. In its regular publication, *The Skilled Tradesman,* United Auto Workers members discuss issues within the industry; however, these issues are firmly located in the wider context. Special-topic publications centering on particular disputes are produced as required, but the I.S.T.C. is also involved in more structured educational activities, such as seminars and workshops, often in conjunction with activist groups from other sections of industry.

This educational activity is directly linked to action. Throughout its history, the I.S.T.C. has actively involved members in leafleting, mass meetings, strike activity, and so on. Further, while criticism of union leadership is an important component of the Council's publicity, the principal thrust of its efforts is directed against the major motor companies and the politicians. The I.S.T.C. is thus both a political and an educational organization, which is itself firmly located within a section of the working-class movement. Its effectiveness is a product of its integration into the struggles of auto workers and of the educational approaches adopted by its leadership. To us, it seems to be a very good illustration of the social change educational model we outlined earlier.

Labor Education and International Solidarity. Our final example concerns another North American activity, a U.S. labor delegation to Nicaragua. In November 1983, eleven American unionists visited Nicaragua to meet union people in that country. They talked with union officials and factory and plantation workers; they studied social services and educational projects. They also took care to ensure that they made contact with a range of labor opinion; thus, they met with the C.U.S., a non-Sandinista union body, an organization that has close links to the A.F.L.-C.I.O., and is the Nicaraguan equivalent of the Chamber of Commerce.

On their return to the U.S., members of the delegation prepared and published an eight-page report in which they outlined their experiences (American Labor Education Center, 1983). They were careful to ensure that they reported not only on the views of the Sandinista-affiliated unions but also on the views of C.U.S. The report is a good example of printed educational material. It deals with those aspects of everyday life that are relevant to working people, regardless of the country in which they live. It provides a factory gate view of life in Nicaragua after Somoza and of what it means to working people; the report documents in tangible ways how things have changed. As union activists living in a third country, we have learned a great deal from this report. The people who went to Nicaragua appear to be credible unionists; the report is tempered and informative. As labor educators, we were struck by the pedagogical soundness of the document; it has been read by many working people in our country simply because it discusses in a credible way issues that our people feel strongly about.

Again, such material can best be used as a discussion starter. By making the link between the issues concerning Nicaragua and working people in an industrial country, the report helps to promote international solidarity. It helps readers to focus on the common character of the issues; readers can inject their own experiences into the discussion. Thus, a dialogue develops around the circumstances that give rise to situations such as those in Central America.

Some Conclusions

We hope that the preceding case studies highlighted some specific how-to's that educators may find useful. In these concluding remarks, we want to focus on some common themes that point to general guidelines for involvement in social change education.

First, each of the educators in the case studies had engaged in some social analysis. It is absolutely essential for those who wish to involve themselves in social change education to engage in some self-education, to tackle difficult, fundamental, theoretical problems, such as the ones we touched on earlier in this chapter. As Paulo Freire (1981) has often noted, liberating education involves reflection as well as action.

Second, each of the educators in the case studies began from where he or she was. We are convinced that the world in which we all live is a world of contradictions, one in which cracks and spaces do open up. The challenge is to recognize opportunities and then have the courage to exploit them.

Third, it seems to us that dialogue was a common theme of all the case studies. In different ways, the educators in our case studies entered into dialogue with the people with whom they wished to work. In this sense, the educators developed a dialogical relationship with everyday struggles.

A British educator, Richard Johnson, put these ideas very aptly when he talked about the need to be actively educative: "Being actively educative is not just a question of 'carrying a policy to the public' or destroying myths about education; it involves learning, too. It involves really listening to popular experiences of formal education. It involves research centering around particular struggles and local issues. It involves making links with other agencies — researchers, community activists, black groups, women's groups — not to take them over, but to learn from their experiences" (Giroux, 1983, p. 238).

Johnson's last point helps us pull together one of the themes that we have been developing in this chapter: Liberating education has very little to do with the enterprise of continuing education that is so often defined and described in the textbooks and even in professional publications, such as this New Directions sourcebook. Liberating education occurs within the context of everyday life; it involves learning associated with the struggle to survive in a world that is not organized in the interests of the majority.

It follows from this that the real educators are not necessarily those whose job titles describe them as such. Throughout our communities, at every level of popular struggle, there are people who are simultaneously educators and learners. These people are the natural allies of those who are formally described as educators and who wish to engage in social change education. Thus, the key question is not really, How can we involve others in social change education? It is, How can we as educators usefully involve ourselves in social change?

References

American Labor Education Center. *Face to Face: An Inside View of Labor in Nicaragua.* Washington: American Labor Education Center, 1983.

Apple, M. W. *Ideology and Curriculum.* London: Routledge & Kegan Paul, 1979.

Bourdieu, P., and Passeron, J. C. *Reproduction in Education, Society, and Culture.* Beverly Hills, Calif.: Sage, 1977.

Bowles, S., and Gintis, H. *Schooling in Capitalist America.* New York: Basic Books, 1976.

Darkenwald, G. G., and Merriam, S. B. *Adult Education: Foundations of Practice.* New York: Harper & Row, 1982.

Freire, P. *Pedagogy of the Oppressed.* New York: Continuum, 1981.

Gelpi, E. *Lifelong Learning: Principles, Policies, and Practice.* Manchester: Manchester University, 1979.

Giroux, H. A. *Ideology, Culture, and the Process of Schooling.* Philadelphia: Temple Press, 1981.

Giroux, H. A. *Theory and Resistance in Education.* South Hadley: Bergin and Garvey, 1983.

Heller, A. "The Emotional Division of Labor Between the Sexes: Perspectives on Feminism and Socialism." *Thesis Eleven,* 1982, 5-6, 59-71.

Law, M. G., and Sissons, L. E. "The Individual, Human Needs, and Social Change: Towards a Reconceptualization." Paper presented at the Rekindling Commitment Conference, Rutgers University, New Brunswick, N.J., June 10-13, 1984.

Puawai: YMCA S.T.E.P.S. Programme. "Assumptions, Objectives, and Course Content." In W. Lee (Ed.), *Puawai.* Unpublished report. Hamilton, New Zealand: Continuing Education Project, University of Waikato, 1984.

Shor, I. *Critical Teaching and Everyday Life.* Boston: Southend Press, 1980.

Sissons, L. E., and Harbridge, R. "Making and Using Video in Trade Union Education." Paper presented at *e ako mo nga ra kei mua* (Learning for Our Future) conference, Wellington, New Zealand, September 1984.

Sissons, L. E., and Law, M. G. "Adaption or Change: The Social Purpose of Continuing Education." *Continuing Education in New Zealand,* 1982, *14* (1), 47-66.

Taumarunui Work Trust. "Proving Everybody Wrong." Videotape documentary, 1983.

Thompson, J. L. (Ed.) *Adult Education for a Change.* London: Hutchinson, 1980.

Thompson, J. L. *Learning Liberation: Women's Response to Men's Education.* London: Croom Helm, 1983.

Michael Law is an adult educator at the University of Waikato, Hamilton, New Zealand.

Linda Sissons directs research and information services for the New Zealand Federation of Labor.

In guided learning engagements, interactions create a passage of thought and speech leading to change.

Mediation as a Helping Presence in Cultural Institutions

David Carr

Each of us discovers and inhabits one life, striving to conduct its course over time and through experience, according to what our habitat contains and requires. "The world," Martin Buber (1947, p. 89) writes, "engenders the person in the individual." Experience educates. Our learning is "a selection . . . of the effective world" (p. 89), and it occurs to us through an instrumental connection between human beings: "First, a relation of no matter what kind, between two persons, second, an event experienced by them in common, in which at least one of them actively participates, and, third, the fact that this one person, without forfeiting anything of the felt reality of his activity, at the same time lives through the common event from the standpoint of the other" (Buber, 1947, p. 97).

The kind of engagement described by Buber—facing another— is a formative human encounter with meaning, because it establishes a continuity or wholeness across the experiences of two persons. Such continuity is at the center of all relationships in which one person strives to imagine the meanings and needs of a different person while feeling no less important meanings and needs of his or her own. This relationship

S. H. Rosenblum (Ed.). *Involving Adults in the Educational Process.* New Directions for Continuing Education, no. 26. San Francisco: Jossey-Bass, June 1985.

occurs when thoughtful, nurturant help is given to a learner, especially when one adult assists another to interpret the messages of experience and independent inquiry.

The word that titles this chapter, *mediation,* is used to mean a relation for learning or continuity between two persons in which one is an instrument or agent of the other's need. The chapter suggests some elements and general conditions of this relation in any setting; libraries and museums are the places where my own understanding of mediated learning began. Clearly, mediated learning is the normative encounter in libraries. Traditional public libraries are model environments for the mode of education that I am thinking about.

Museums offer a different and less explicit form of mediation in their public messages: maps and labels, printed guides or handbooks, the organization of the physical environment itself—all these offer messages to learners. And, in some museums—for example, the Exploratorium in San Francisco—mediators or "explainers" are present to assist museum users. Reconstructions, such as those in Williamsburg and Plymouth, also use persons to mediate learning. Whatever the setting and level of assistance, satisfactory learning in any cultural institution is unlikely to be random; wherever it is encountered, the order of things and experiences conveys mediation—the useful exchange of guiding messages between human beings.

Unfortunately, explicit mediation or designed helping given to individual learners over time in public learning environments has become encapsulated in routines and programs that are almost accidental parts of what these institutions are about. Sustained individual encounters for learning in the museum or the library—moments when two persons face each other with a shared question—are rare. We might say that, under the somewhat unthinking assumption that wherever people learn they must somehow be instructed, public language often replaces private messages in cultural institutions. Ivan Illich (1977, p. 1) describes this step away from conviviality: "Fifty years ago, most of the words an American heard were personally spoken to him as an individual or to somebody standing nearby. Only occasionally did words reach him as an undifferentiated member of a crowd—in the classroom or in church, at a rally or a circus. Words were mostly like handwritten, sealed letters and not like the junk that now pollutes our mails. Today, words that are directed to one person's attention have become rare." We are, quite literally, at a loss for words, especially language meant for us as adults and for our lives as adult learners.

A Definition of Mediation

Messages that reach us about our choices as learners amid all the public and quasi-public noises surrounding our lives are words of an entirely unusual kind. They are nonroutine messages that assist us to think and decide, to see ourselves, to become informed, more competent, better able to sort experiences and sift their meanings, less disabled by the loud words coming from surrounding machines. Mediative messages also cause us to be more self-defined, less defined by the junk messages of our culture. They are meant exactly for us, from our lovers, mentors, caregivers, and nurturing others.

Whatever the origin of the nurturing voice, messages intended for one learner are radical messages, because as they reduce or clarify complexities, they also help to define the learner in relation to a task. For example, the voices of cultural institutions can guide the learner toward a question that is fitting or an experience that is informing. Such messages also include resonant gifts of process, tools, and encouragement meant for the learner alone. In our society, only libraries and museums exist to offer messages of this kind. Of course, institutions have voices only metaphorically. In truth, institutional messages come from the personal choices and actions of individual helpers in their relations with the persons they help.

When a learner's experiences are mediated by another person, the nature of immediate — that is, of directly experienced — knowledge is changed. The quality of the relation between the mediator and the learner has its own powerful substance, form, and presence. The first meanings of mediation, as Raymond Williams (1976, p. 170) points out, refer to "a means of transmission, or agency as a medium." He adds (p. 171) that "it is not the neutral process of the interaction of separate forms but an active process in which the form of the mediation alters the things mediated or by its nature indicates their nature." Mediation — I now use the word to mean guided learning in cultural institutions — bestows coherent and useful form on the learner's experience. To a learner in the complex processes of change, a mediator is a bridge or a designer of bridges.

Mediation for Change. Allen Tough (1982) suggests that an approach to foster change has four steps: first, helping someone toward an aware and knowing understanding of change, a realistic image of self and path; second, helping someone to see and manage the effectiveness of natural change processes in one life; third, helping someone to assess intentions and arrive at a fitting design; fourth, helping someone to recognize and act on the need for assistance in the future. These four intentions fit within the descriptions of helping found in the works of others. Ralph Brockett (1983) has summarized these recently.

Because public cultural institutions—libraries, museums—are invitational environments, attractive to people by their contents and messages, mediation can be seen as a personal extension of the public invitation offered. Its messages are more like the handwritten letters in Illich's description than the manipulative demands of schools or the electronic marketplace. That these relationships are personal is clear. A person brings private experiences to the objects and texts of a cultural institution and with them a host of meanings, memories, and values. The mediating voice centers on these personal dimensions and on the connections between these images and the learning environment. These connections are invitational because they engender inquiry; they lead the learner on. In such passages, even complexities and obstacles invite the learner to reimagine, restate, or renew the goals and values of the learning task. A cultural institution offers the learner new configurations of data; mediation is its process of offering.

Over time—often brief, sometimes extended—an alliance for learning can emerge between two persons. Useful experiences are designed. Choices and evaluations occur. Dimensions of order, expectation, consistency, and stability appear as the alliance becomes more sensitive to the learner's directions. Mediation aids this system-sensitivity by emphasizing the process of learning, rather than its product, and by sorting the patterns of experience. These qualities of order are instrumental, not ephemeral. Useful mediation lasts as a memorable, informing presence, and so it goes beyond information to affect the learning process itself. By touching the conditions and patterns of learning in an adult life, mediation alters experience and nurtures change in the person.

Visible Elements, Invisible Ambiguities. Any learning that occurs in a cultural institution can be characterized by its clarities, implications, and ambiguities. And, because the means of learning change, these characteristics are not constant. The visible elements of an encounter for learning in a library, for example, might be clear at first: Two actors are present (librarian, learner), a question is asked (about human evolution, for example), a reference tool or process is selected (encyclopedias, books), and tasks follow (reading, documentation, thought). But, topics may shift by becoming more specific (paleoanthropology), more personal (Charles Darwin), or more applied (textbook controversies). Tools and texts may change, or they may be enhanced by objects, films, or tapes; if they do, the learner's tasks change. Of these several visible elements, only the presence of the two invested actors is continuous, and even they do not remain the same persons throughout the task.

The invisible elements of such encounters are even more mutable; they change subtly and silently. These, too, may be clear at first; there is a relationship for learning between two individuals, a stated goal between them. An objective is determined, an attitude is present; expectations may appear, and attention is fixed on the task. But, goals change as experience broadens, objectives are revised or abandoned, attitudes mature, expectations meet reality, and attention wanders. These are necessary parts of an alliance for learning. Of the invisible elements that may be clear as an encounter for learning begins, only one remains at its close: the relations between two persons engaged in the work at hand—and that bond has probably experienced some weathering of its own.

It is difficult to guide or mediate a learner's experience for several reasons. First, such engagements demand skills that most people— including librarians and museum educators—are rarely encouraged or explicitly helped to learn. Second, because they include exceedingly personal messages, these are social relationships; they have values, meanings, and even intimacies that go beyond the exchanges of information on which they center. Third, these are examples of interdependency, and they create bonds. Fourth, these encounters are demanding. On the one hand, they require responsiveness, adaptation, and pliancy. On the other, they demand accuracy, information, and strength. Fifth, they assist what Ronald Havelock (1977) calls "process helping," the focus of which is invisible and consequently difficult to define. Finally, while engaging in these dynamic acts of mediation, the mediator continues to be an agent of the invitational environment. Every helping act must be generically inviting, regardless of stressful circumstances.

The ambiguities of such encounters are numberless; a small list is likely to suggest others. For example, the helping alliance is typically founded on a need in the learner and on an implied strength in the helper. Under such an implication, it is difficult for a helper to be baffled for long. Alliances for learning are mutual and collaborative; they bind two individuals together. While the resulting relationships are likely to be positive, they also reduce autonomy; at times, it may be difficult to feel free. Yet, despite this proximity, some unknowns between partners (feelings, fears, distant goals) can remain private and inaccessible. The most pervasive ambiguity of the helping relationship lies in the learner's absolute freedom to ignore the help offered. However unformed the learner's powers may be, they can be strong enough to resist suggestions from the most persuasive advocate.

Communication in Mediation

The great challenge to mediation is not the ambiguity or difficulty of assistance, although these pose formidable challenges. Rather, it is the lasting stress of giving effective personal messages in an impersonal environment.

The Content of Messages. The messages of mediation are both public and private. The public words are not difficult, but they are also not perfunctory. For example, learning engagements in cultural institutions have several concrete objectives, and these can be clarified in words: determining the topic and then developing a plan that includes a time plan, an approach to data, and a sequence of experiences. Although these aspects of guided experience may appear to be relatively shallow, they are important because they set limits and create reasonable expectations. They are important as well, because they elicit commitment and confirmation from the learner. Pragmatic limits also help to determine the initial boundaries and levels of mediation and the purposes of the learning plan. Early clarifications are also useful when it is time to close and evaluate.

More abstract, private intentions are necessary as well, and they are not easy to capture in words. These objectives have to do with the depth of an inquiry, the learner's assumptions of autonomy and control, and the qualities of balance, design, and proportion. It is possible to think of these intentions as esthetic aspects of the learning encounter having to do with imagination, flow, continuity, and the pleasures of connoisseurship. Often, they are unspoken. These are the aspects of mediation that move toward art and feeling and away from definition and function.

There is also an internal architecture in learning relationships having to do with supportive themes and meanings and with connections to other experiences or topics. What are the intended and unintended consequences of this work? What are its pleasures, surprises, or disappointments? What does it mean to one life as an entity?

Language Transforming Experience. It is important to understand mediation as an act of language, as a deep engagement of listening, feeling, attending, and expressing in ways that are useful to learning. Two aspects of the brilliant work done by Lev Vygotsky (1962, 1978) in the early part of this century may have implications for our understanding both of the relationship of mediator and learner and of the role of language in that connection. Although Vygotsky's work is largely about child cognition, the power of his ideas makes them worth suggesting in the adult context.

It is clear that, in common speech, words capture a number of meanings and qualities, denotative and connotative, about experience. Vygotsky (1962, p. 153) summarizes the effect of words on experience: "The relation between thought and word is a living process; thought is born through words. A word devoid of thought is a dead thing, and a thought unembodied in words remains a shadow. The connection between them, however, is not a preformed and constant one. It emerges in the course of development, and itself evolves. . . . Words play a central part not only in the development of thought but in the historical growth of consciousness as a whole."

Language is an instrument through which thought takes form, through which it can be shared, examined, reconsidered, and changed. Language itself changes thought by taking it from the realm of inner speech, where it is an unknown territory, and moving it slowly into words, an accessible realm. This transformation emphasizes the place of language at the center of our operations as learners. Language constructs thinking, helps to possess it in communicable forms, and permits critical examination of the course of inquiry. Before it is anything else, mediation is an act of change or transformation through language, a convergence of thinking and speaking. Dewey (1933) and Bruner (1975) also offer important discussions of language and thinking. It is likely that there is much to be learned about mediation by examining the discourses and subtexts of real encounters.

Vygotsky (1978, p. 86) also posited the existence of a realm he called the *zone of proximal development*. The zone of proximal development is the difference between actual, independent performance on a task and performance under expert guidance or "in collaboration with more capable peers." The zone of proximal development defines learning that is in progress, emerging but not yet mature. Interaction helps to expand skills by inviting the learner to reach for a higher—more organized or more coherent—level of thought. In Vygotsky's (1978, p. 90) words, "learning awakens a variety of internal developmental processes that are able to operate only when the [learner] is interacting with people in his environment and in cooperation with his peers. Once these processes are internalized, they become part of the [learner's] independent developmental achievement."

This idea begins to capture the quality of the invitation offered by the mediator in the cultural institution. It is an invitation to use language in an effort to transform unexpressed thought and experience into coherent knowing. It is also an invitation to enter the proximal zone of development, where, in an engagement with another person, the learner's potential but unformed powers can be evoked and possessed.

As I have done elsewhere (Carr, 1983), I want to make connections between learning engagements in cultural institutions and the theory of mediated learning experience advanced by Reuven Feuer-stein (1980). Feuerstein's work, like Vygotsky's, is aimed at modifying the learning of children, specifically of culturally deprived learners for whom the processes of cultural transmission are incomplete; cultural deprivation has "reduced [the] propensity of the individual to organize and elaborate stimuli to facilitate their future use by means of mental processes (Feuerstein, 1980, p. 15). Feuerstein's ideas can be applied to the construction of adult learning, especially in relation to mediation. "We conceive of the development of cognitive structure in the organism as a product of two modalities of interaction between the organism and its environment: direct exposure to sources of stimuli and mediated learning" (Feuerstein, 1980, p. 15).

The meaning of direct exposure to sources of stimuli in cultural institutions is clear: The use of books, objects, texts, artifacts, and other examples is easily documented and widely experienced. The second modality in Feuerstein's definition, mediated learning, refers to "the way in which stimuli emitted by the environment are transformed by a 'mediating' agent. . . [who,] guided by his intentions, culture, and emotional investment, selects and organizes the world of stimuli for the [learner]" (Feuerstein, 1980, pp. 15–16). By this designed intervention of framing and filtering by an invested other, the structures and patterns of intellectual experience are altered: "Mediated learning experience may be conceptualized as inducing in the organism a great variety of orientations and strategies that become crystallized in the form of sets and habits. . . not merely the transmission of specific skills or abilities but the development of the prerequisite cognitive schemata to enable an individual to derive maximum benefit from direct exposure to sources of stimulation" (Feuerstein, 1980, pp. 16–17, 19).

Edward de Bono's (1970) image of the mind as a pattern-making environment is strikingly supportive here. Think, for example, of the mind and the museum as two permeable environments, each offering patterns of meaning to the other. Recent research says that this kind of intelligence does not diminish, even with advanced age. "Accumulating data have firmly shown that one key mental faculty, called crystallized intelligence, continues to rise over the life span in healthy, active people. . . . Crystallized intelligence is a person's ability to use an accumulated body of general information to make judgments and solve problems" (Goleman, 1984, p. C1). Mediation intended to enhance this construct-inducing faculty appears to be important among adult learners in any setting, but its applications in cultural institutions, where limitless data lie unconstructed waiting for the learner, seem especially compelling.

Assisting the Passage Across Experience

Mediation alters experience. Instrumental alliances enhance the focus and coherence of adult learning in cultural environments. Much of this coherence occurs because the relation between mediator and learner takes the form of language in conversation and dialogue. Thus, it appears that one critical need for this form of learning has to do with capturing that language in useful ways. Forms of documentation — notes, journals, commonplace books, free-association exercises, tape-recorded monologues, cognitive maps, and other visual images — would be simple but practical ways of recording the language of emerging thoughts. "A thought," Vygotsky (1962, p. 150) writes, "may be compared to a cloud shedding a shower of words."

But, documentation cannot capture the most distinctive and richest qualities of learning in this relationship, which have to do with what Buber (1947) refers to as living through a common event from the standpoint of another person. For example, as a mediator in my own teaching I have seen learners experience explosions of information that falls into broad patterns over a wide range — and implosions of information that falls into narrow but deep channels. I have also seen learners feel and react to the sustaining cycles of intensity and play that occur to the best inquirers over time. Finally, I have seen the end of an inquiry turn suddenly toward new questions, which is to say that, when one learning invitation has been satisfied, others appear. Mediation in its best form means that one is both a witness to and a participant in the presence of another's learning and also in the emergence of inviting new unknowns.

References

Brockett, R. "Facilitator Roles and Skills." *Lifelong Learning: The Adult Years,* 1983, *6* (5), 7-9.

Bruner, J. S. "Language as an Instrument of Thought." In A. Davies (Ed.), *Problems of Language and Learning.* London: Heinemann, 1975.

Buber, M. *Between Man and Man.* London: Routledge & Kegan Paul, 1947.

Carr, D. "Adult Learning and Library Helping." *Library Trends,* 1983, *31* (4), 569-583.

de Bono, E. *Lateral Thinking.* New York: Harper & Row, 1970.

Dewey, J. *How We Think.* Lexington, Mass.: Heath, 1933.

Feuerstein, R. *Instrumental Enrichment: An Intervention Program for Cognitive Modifiability.* Baltimore, Md.: University Park Press, 1980.

Goleman, D. "The Aging Mind Proves Capable of Lifelong Growth." *New York Times,* February 21, 1984, pp. C1, C5.

Havelock, R. G. "Information Professionals as Change Agents." *Drexel Library Quarterly,* 1977, *13* (2), 48-61.

Illich, I. *Toward a History of Needs.* New York: Pantheon, 1977.

96

Tough, A. *Intentional Changes*. Chicago: Follett, 1982.

Vygotsky, L. S. *Thought and Language*. Cambridge, Mass.: M.I.T. Press, 1962.

Vygotsky, L. S. *Mind in Society*. Cambridge, Mass.: Harvard University Press, 1978.

Williams, R. *Keywords: A Vocabulary of Culture and Society*. New York: Oxford University Press, 1976.

David Carr teaches adult educators about cultural institutions and lifelong learning at the Graduate School of Education, Rutgers University. A grant from the Rutgers University Research Council has helped to support his recent work on thinking and learning in American cultural institutions.

*The teacher must see the adult learner as adjunct faculty with
personal experience that can be applied to the topic.*

Reflections of a
Teacher of Adults

Jonathan A. Freedman

The teacher enters the first class in introductory sociology. He states
unequivocally to his adult students, "Put on your coats, we're leaving."
He then takes them on a sociological tour of the neighborhood surrounding the classroom building.

The teacher walks into another class and states, "The criminal
justice system is like an animal; the police are its eyes and ears, the
prison its belly. Who will play the eyes? The belly? Let us arrest anyone
who is late to class and have them deal with this beast of the system."

The teacher states, "I want you each to make a paper airplane
and embellish it; make it yours." Before the exercise is done, the class
members explore organizational design and the meaning of craft and
industrial revolution.

A student describes his stress world to the class. The instructor
has students play the people and concepts that are stress producing.
When the student hears a phrase that brings on the stress, those
observing see the student's reaction to stress.

The teacher states, "I don't want you to write a term paper.
Please create a game that demonstrates your understanding of a social
problem." The teacher plays each game with the student to understand

S. H. Rosenblum (Ed.). *Involving Adults in the Educational
Process.* New Directions for Continuing Education, no. 26.
San Francisco: Jossey-Bass, June 1985.

whether the student has grasped the conceptual framework of the problem and to determine a grade.

The teacher creates a Tinkertoy model of a new hospital record-keeping system to make the parts of the system visible. Trainees, who are rather hostile toward the new system, laugh at the strange contraption, especially when it falls apart "accidentally."

These are some of the inventions that help me motivate adults to learn. What I know comes from eighteen years of teaching and thinking about teaching across the spectrum of adult learners, ranging from adults in evening colleges to adults in training workshops. I teach staff in state hospitals, employees in corporations, students in academic settings, prisoners, and citizens of many communities. I also have designed programs for training adults that others teach. I teach a wide range of subjects: sociology, criminology, human resource management, stress management, dealing with difficult people, biopsychosocial theory, and health ethics.

My Mentors as Models

I have been taught in my career by some exemplary teachers. I can see their influence in what I do. At times, when I am faced with a difficult teaching problem, I invoke teaching images of one or more of the teachers in my personal pantheon and think through how that exemplar might handle the problem. Their teaching styles ranged from the quiet to the dramatic, from nondirective to highly directive. Why do I perceive them as exemplars? I believe it to be because they saw me as a person and because they could recognize, relate to, and help me to enhance my own learning style regardless of external situational factors, such as the size of the class, the need to grade, or my challenges to the usual rules of learning: flaunting deadlines, doing unusual assignments, or appearing to sleep in class.

These teachers motivated me by encouraging me to do my own thinking, treating me not only as a junior member of a community of scholars but also as an adult capable of making my own decisions and determining my responsibilities. They never totally abandoned me when I did not do what they thought I should do. I also benefited by learning from these teachers in a college and at graduate schools that were small in size and that allowed for considerable individualization. The practices of my mentors have been absorbed into my own teaching style. I try to transmit some of the quality, individuation, and intensity I felt in my own education into whatever teaching-learning situation I enter regardless of the class size or supposed ability of the students. I share with my mentors a passion for teaching, especially for communicating clearly, and a commitment to lifelong learning.

Helping People to Learn Is the Art of Teaching

The usual student I face as a teacher is either an adult who is motivated enough to want to gain further education at the end of a working day or one who is required to come to a training program. Except for the limited teaching I do as part of my main job, I also am teaching at the end of eight hours of work. Of course, it is easier for me to lecture at students, limit discussion, and hope that my tired charm, charisma, experience, and erudition will keep people awake and interested. I can relish the power of controlling the attention of many in the group. In exchange, they have learned how to demonstrate by little signs that they understand. I am happy that they appear to be learning, but are they really? When I ask for questions, most keep quiet. I think I must be getting through. Does the fact that they ask few questions mean that they understand? Frequently, when I get formal feedback for grading purposes, I find that many students have not grasped some of the basic concepts from my presentations.

Why is that? Am I a poor lecturer? Are the students too stupid to learn? Is my testing device not related to my goals and objectives? I tend to lecture well. When the students talk, they seem to be bright. The testing devices I use are open-ended; they give students several choices for demonstrating their learning. I state and restate what I am looking for with great frequency. Something else must be wrong. I conclude that for adults the art of teaching is helping people to learn. The teacher must be a tour guide who starts at the beginning of the knowledge trip and moves with the students past twists and turns, through thickets and onto peaks. The teacher must be a catalyst providing sturctured activities that involve the student in learning. The teacher must see the adult learner as adjunct faculty with personal experience that can be applied to the topic. The teacher must accept these experiences positively without arrogance. Therefore, the learning climate must be quite open with minimal control, yet the teacher must make it clear that more directive teaching styles will be used on occasion.

The teacher actively demonstrates patience, flexibility, and critical support. The teacher also shows that he or she can make a mistake. This frequently requires what I term the *one-down strategy:* I make it clear that I don't know everything, that there is room for their learning to take place, that their ideas on how they wish to demonstrate mastery of the topic will be encouraged, and that I am learning from them. The teacher must also demonstrate that he or she can be in charge of the situation when necessary, that he or she is taking a specific approach to allow for learning and interaction with every student. I believe that as I teach I empower students to be effective learners, to take charge of their education.

Shy Learners and Dominating Learners

Shyness has reached epidemic proportions among adult learners. Many students are afraid to engage the teacher or reveal themselves to classmates. They give the impression that they are sitting with their mouths open ready to ingest knowledge pablum, a magic cereal that enhances career options; the only hard work involved is having to agree with the teacher. When I explore such shyness with a student, he or she can often trace it to an early experience when a teacher made fun of a response or allowed other students to critique the student's unprepared performance. Adults bring to the classroom residues of their earlier education; frequently, early education has taught them that the teacher is an authority with superior knowledge and power to maintain order and that blind obedience is required. I believe that the teacher who uses a confrontational strategy toward any student creates a fear in others that he or she will treat them the same without warning. I seldom use a confrontational strategy in my teaching and then only after I share why I am doing this with my students.

I see far fewer adults who try to dominate the class. My model of openness makes it hard for me to silence those who dominate. I wait patiently for the other members of the class to reinforce the norm of shared time. When I grow impatient, I talk to the offender outside class.

Preparation

I approach each class by thinking through the goals that I wish to accomplish and learning activities that might help me to accomplish these goals. I seldom use extensive notes. Each class must be an improvisation within this goal structure. I must be able to adjust to the concerns of the learners, moving or changing my strategies to respond to their needs. The difficulty is not to allow oneself to go off on perpetual tangents in response to learners' questions. I want to be able to move on or come back to topics that I believe need to be covered, but I realize that there is more than one way of bringing about learning. I have learned from student evaluations that my degree of preparation is not the major factor in the quality of my teaching. It appears to be how well I aid students to take responsibility for their own learning. Frequently, I believe I am teaching a way of thinking about oneself in the context of organization, community, and society. I find that students need to begin by practicing the basic skills of looking, listening, questioning, reporting, and thinking critically. I used to assume that students already knew how to do this, but I have learned that practice is necessary. I try and build such practice into my preparation.

How Does This Work Out in the Classroom?

At the beginning of an adult class, I must learn whether students are ready to learn or whether they are still dealing with the residue of what happened earlier in the day. I try to use an exercise that orients adult learners to the present. This exercise can involve learning the names of other students, exchanging positive occurrences that have taken place since the last meeting, or presenting mild upsets. I am influenced by the approach called *Re-evaluation counseling,* which uses short-term exchanges of time between two persons as a powerful technique in teaching and counseling. The student dyads can function simultaneously so that in less than ten minutes all students can work through their residues and be open to learning. Co-counseling also gives training in the basic skills of looking, listening, questioning, and reporting as well as in understanding the perspective of another person.

After an opening, I present my agenda for the class and ask for suggestions or modifications. If it is going to be a long class, I sometimes ask someone to be in charge of when the break should come. This student's job is to sense the condition of class members and announce the break.

I try to vary my approach by having several thirty-minute segments in each class. I choose among lecture, discussion, game or simulation, audiovisual programs, short field observations, guest demonstrations, small-group exercises, co-counseling exchanges on particular topics, individual reflection that sometimes leads to short presentations shared with the group, and metateaching, which shares with the class why I am doing what I do. While I might have thought through the likely segments and a possible order in advance, what actually happens is determined as the class takes place.

I try to get everyone to participate in some manner during every class. My goal in large classes is to find ways of providing the range of experiences that can take place in a small class. I try to praise students for their ideas and questions, not as a ritual but often. I do not put students down; I try to work with students who seem not to understand by asking for their ideas and showing alternatives.

I use humor. However, I do not tell jokes well. When I was evaluated by students in my prison class, I was told not even to attempt to tell jokes. My style tends to use wit and word play. This approach keeps laughter in the classroom.

I usually have a learning party for an ongoing class. The party is a mix of cooperative dinner and guest speaker. I also continue classes after their official ending time by meeting for pizza and beverages. These activities break down the distance between learners and teacher. However, I still maintain some distance; we all know that I must evaluate student performance. I have become a mentor for several students, and I am still in touch with students from my first class.

I believe that such contact continues because we are like people who have been on a journey together. We have shared the rewards of reaching a destination with increased knowledge, changed attitudes, and new competencies.

Jonathan A. Freedman is director of education and training at Hutchings Psychiatric Institute. He is affiliated with the Department of Sociology at Syracuse University. He was voted teacher of the year by students at Syracuse's University College in 1984.

*Educators must begin to relinquish exclusive control over the
learning situation and encourage autonomy in learners.*

The Adult Learner: Central to the Planning-Learning Process

Sandra H. Rosenblum

The authors of the chapters in this volume have varied backgrounds
and points of view, but each is struggling in his or her own way with the
issue of involving adults more deeply and more meaningfully in the
educational process. What clearly emerges from these chapters is the
strong desire of the authors to witness an alteration in traditional
educator-learner relationships and roles. If one can extract a theme
from the contributions to this volume, it is that, if the adult learner is to
become central to the planning-learning process, educators must begin
to relinquish their exclusive control over the learning situation and
encourage the learner's autonomy.

As the role of the learner increases in planning and decision making, the role of the instructor is inevitably transformed so that he or she
becomes more a partner in the process of learning and less the source of
all knowledge.

The transformation in consciousness that occurs when a parent
begins to relinquish authority over maturing adolescents parallels in
many ways the changes that occur when an instructor decides to share
authority in a classroom. It must be acknowledged that the task of let-
ting go can be fraught with as much anxiety for educators of adults as it
may be for parents of adolescents.

S. H. Rosenblum (Ed.). *Involving Adults in the Educational
Process.* New Directions for Continuing Education, no. 26.
San Francisco: Jossey-Bass, June 1985.

As the youngster's autonomy increases, parents must confront the anxiety that emerges when they no longer take care of the child's every need. Similarly, the instructor of adults who has expanded the learner's role will need to work against the anxiety that no longer serving as the sole provider of all knowledge and information engenders. The fear that parents experience when they feel that perhaps they have granted too much too soon will be matched by the apprehension of educators who may long for the old, safer methods that assured them of total control.

In both situations, the results of relinquishing authority seem to be worth the risks. Parents usually heave a sigh of relief when their children become independent, self-sufficient adults. And, if we can assume that the authors of the chapters in this volume are representative of the field, continuing educators seem eager to accept adult students more as involved partners in the educational process than as passive recipients.

Several chapters explore the shift in learner and educator roles as a means of increasing student involvement. Freedman characterizes the successful educator as one who learns from his or her students and who helps students to take responsibility for their own education. Carr's guide serves a similar role. According to Carr, a relationship between learner and guide develops when the guide is able to assist another to interpret messages of experience and independent inquiry. Niemi contends that, even in the highly structured institutional mode of education where learning is strictly content centered, learners can still participate if the teacher understands the unique characteristics of adult learners and brings them into play by using appropriate methods and techniques. And, Vedros suggests that continuing educators use a practical technique that can transform the adult learner into an active participant in the planning of programs.

Law and Sissons offer yet another perspective on the learner-educator relationship in their chapter on distance education. They make the point that, even when educator and learner are face to face, their relationship may be very "distant" if the structure of the educational program is nonnegotiable or if there is no opportunity for dialogue. Conversely, distance can become relatively insignificant if a close, egalitarian relationship is established with the instructor through a program with a clear negotiable structure and opportunities for feedback and dialogue. The chapter emphasizes the need for developing technologies that will maximize dialogue and learner autonomy. Existing technologies emphasize only the setting of objectives and the structuring of knowledge.

Ilsley offers an additional criticism of existing educational technology as a barrier to learner participation in literacy programs. He blames the field's inadequate tools for the failure of literacy programs to address such learner concerns as poverty and unemployment. In Ilsley's vision of a successful literacy program, the role of the educator is transformed from keeper of technology into facilitator of dialogue.

The use of discussion and dialogue as a method for involving adults in the learning process is a recurrent theme in the volume. The chapter by Law and Sissons on social change presents a number of case studies in which, in different ways, the educators developed a dialogical relationship with learners in order to comprehend and evaluate everyday struggles. Brookfield sees participation in discussion, in the sense of a willingness to examine the origins of one's beliefs and to view one's meaning systems as provisional and relative, as a method of truly realizing one's adulthood.

Clearly, much significant thinking and writing about involving adults in the educational process has taken place. However, we still have much to learn about this topic, which profoundly affects our practice as continuing educators. As Rosenblum concludes in Chapter Two, for us to be able to make meaningful assertions about the effects of participation on our educational programs, substantially more thought and research are required. The benefits to our practice will be well worth the effort.

Sandra H. Rosenblum is director of education and training at the New York State Psychiatric Institute. She teaches classes in adult education at the Graduate School of Education, Rutgers University.

Index